Praise for *Creating Your Own Destiny*

"More Americans put families ahead of work. Family is important to Patrick Snow. He is a speaker, coach, and author of *Creating Your Own Destiny*. Employees used to be willing to sacrifice because of things like stock options. Now they're fed up. They realize that family is the only stabilizing force in today's turbulent economy. Making time for family isn't just important for a few employees like Snow—it's a growing priority for many workers disillusioned by layoffs, corporate scandal, and waning corporate loyalty. Seventy percent of employees don't think there is a healthy balance between work and personal life."

USA TODAY
Cover story, December 5, 2002

"When Patrick Snow, a consultant in Bainbridge Island, WA, decided to leave a corporate sales job he called three friends for advice. 'The employee handbook was good for a general overview, but it failed to answer some specific questions,' said Mr. Snow who left to start his own professional speaking business. 'Lucky for me, the information my buddies gave me enabled me to plan my exit strategy perfectly.'"

The New York Times
Business page, September 4, 2005

"Patrick Snow's *Creating Your Own Destiny* is the most energetic and inspiring book written on fulfilling your dreams and finding true happiness in life. I do not doubt that it will be a classic in the field of self-help beside *Think and Grow Rich* and *The Power of Positive Thinking*."

Tyler Tichelaar
www.SuperiorBookPromotions.com

"I am constantly looking for books that are well-written, resonate with our coaching approach of life-work balance, and that I can recommend to our clients. In writing *Creating Your Own Destiny*, Patrick Snow has produced a book that accomplishes all three. I like his balance between simplicity and insight. The book is a tremendous resource for anyone who wants to get started on living a life with purpose, direction, and fulfillment."

Raymond Gleason,
Executive Coach, Building Champions, Inc.

"The insights in your book are exactly what the people in our country need to live a better life. I am hopeful that I can bring you to Indonesia soon for a seminar. I will be the first to greet you off the plane."

Sanjay Ramchandani
INDONESIA

"Reading *Creating Your Own Destiny* has changed my life. I had all my goals in my mind but I needed your book to show me how to turn all my ideas into action."

Flavia De Angelis
ITALY

"As a result of reading your book two years ago, I have completely re-prioritized my life. At the time I was very confused, so your book was a blessing to me. After seeing you speak live in person, I have realized that now is the time to build my business again."

Elvie Regala
PHILIPPINES

"I think your book is clear, practical, and stimulating. The basic idea that man makes his own destiny is something that all human beings must come to understand."

Rodolfo F. Cordero
ARGENTINA

"Your book is excellent. I particularly enjoyed the part that covers how to create wealth and earn residual income through business ownership. Great work!"

Michael Bullock
IRELAND

"Your book taught me that if I am going to achieve my goals, I must never give up! Your book has been an incredible resource for me in keeping my dreams alive."

Pablo Fritz
PANAMA

"I really benefited from your message in your book about overcoming your self-limiting beliefs. Thanks for sharing this gift with your readers in our country."

Vale Gonzalez
CHILE

"Thanks for the personal touch in writing your great book. I am very impressed as to how you show such a strong interest in the lives of your students. It really puts the cherry on the cake. I want you to remember my name because I will meet you one day."

Lukas Teblanch
SOUTH AFRICA

"If I had the authority in the government of Uganda, I would have you come speak to all of our citizens. Your book and destiny message offers an incredible career road map."

Rwendeire Peniel
UGANDA

"Your book taught me that no one can hold me back except myself. I am now attracting the most amazing opportunities. How enlightening it is to know that I can create and achieve my own destiny."

Merlyn Gibson
NEW ZEALAND

"Your book has helped me realize that all is possible in life. I have been having some rough times at work as of late and your book has helped me overcome this adversity."

Emel Ramirez
COSTA RICA

"Patrick, you have written a tremendous book and you are an amazing speaker. You have a great way of bringing out the best in all of us. After listening to you speak, I walked away creating the best of me!"

A.M. Noel
MALAYSIA

"I have read more than 700 self-help and motivational books and yours is the best! I have read the Spanish version of your book and will apply all that I have learned to my life."

Alberto Hernandez
SPAIN

"Your book is excellent and your speech was the best one of the entire conference! It woke me up to ask myself where I am at this stage of my life. Thank you for the light that you turned back on in my mind. I am again on the horse."

Vladimir Chepurnoi
RUSSIA

"I don't know quite how to describe the full impact that your book has made on my life! It now serves as my life guideline since I have learned that I can indeed overcome all the adversities in my life."

Kelvin Uzomah
NIGERIA

"I am now reading your book a second time and it is the best book I have ever read! Please keep blessing people like myself who are looking for a better way of life."

Karen Harding
JAMAICA

"I just read your incredible book and now I am reading it a second time. It bristles with superb information and my mind is now full of exciting new ideas!"

Peter Thompson
UNITED KINGDOM

"I downloaded your free goals sheets and completed all of the exercises in your book. I am 70 years young and convinced that reading your book has helped me become even more successful. I am not too old to learn from your wonderfully written book."

Brian Eastwood
AUSTRALIA

"I very much enjoyed your book! Your exercises in the book transformed me from someone who was hoping to succeed, to someone who now expects to succeed. What a difference you have made in my life."

Suzanne Alexander
CANADA

"Your book was amazing. I want to create my own destiny and reading your book and hearing you speak was my first step. I was impacted by your energy and passion."

Maggie Williams
UNITED STATES

"May I tell you that you have written a fantastic book and it is helping me in many ways. I am at a stage in my life where I am searching for my destiny and your book has helped me better define my future."

Dan Hodges
UNITED KINGDOM

"I have read all kinds of books that have encouraged me to create my own destiny, but none have worked until I read yours. I am now energized and moving full speed ahead all thanks to your destiny message."

Dennis Ofori-Asiedu
GHANA

"Your book and CD set have really helped me launch my career. You have provided solutions for me that I could not have learned on my own. I hope to meet you one day."

Ohansi Gilbert Okafor
CAMEROON

"Your quote—'Only those who can see the invisible can achieve the impossible. The belief in your vision holds the key to creating your own destiny'—has helped me catapult my business to the next level."

Chis Igwe
FRANCE

"Patrick you are a very inspiring speaker and your book is an incredible gift to mankind. Thanks for helping me through some difficult career choices. I recommend your book to anyone who wants more out of life."

Akio Minami
JAPAN

"I found your book to be very practical. It is like a summary as to how to live a successful life. It is like a life manual. I could not put it down and finished your book in one sitting."

Sanjay Shinde
INDIA

"I must say I found your book to be straight from the heart. I have read many books on goal setting, but found that this particular book definitely hit a chord. Your book is easy to read and I felt as if I could almost hear your voice."

Jerome Patience
SOUTH AFRICA

"After reading your book and seeing you speak, I have been able to claim a new mantra: I am focused, organized and making lots of money! Why? Because you have taught me for whom I really work—my family!"

Jan Zufelt
UNITED STATES

CREATING YOUR OWN DESTINY

How to Get Exactly What You Want Out of Life and Work

PATRICK SNOW

WILEY

John Wiley & Sons, Inc.

Published by John Wiley & Sons, Inc., Hoboken, New Jersey.
Published simultaneously in Canada.

For general information on our other products and services or for technical support,
please contact our Customer Care Department within the United States at (800) 762-2974,
outside the United States at (317) 572-3993 or fax (317) 572-4002.

Wiley also publishes its books in a variety of electronic formats. Some content that appears
in print may not be available in electronic books. For more information about Wiley
products, visit our web site at www.wiley.com.

Library of Congress Cataloging-in-Publication Data:

Snow, Patrick, 1969–
  Creating your own destiny : how to get exactly what you want out of life
and work / by Patrick Snow.
      p. cm.
ISBN: 978-0-470-58202-2 (cloth)
1. Self-actualization (Psychology).   2. Self-realization.   3. Job satisfaction.
4. Success.   I. Title.
BF637.S4S654 2010
650.1—dc22

2010003216

Printed in the United States of America

10 9 8 7 6 5 4 3 2 1

To my beautiful wife, Cheryl: Thank you for being
so supportive of me in my many endeavors over the years!
I appreciate you sticking with me through the good times and bad.
I love you dearly!

To my children, Samuel and Jacob: You are the reason that
I work so hard. This book is written for you. I hope that long
after my time, you and your children will benefit from
this destiny message.
I love you both!

To my parents, Jack and Lois Snow: You are the best parents
a child could ask for. I have become the person I am today
because of you both. Thank you for all the positive words
of encouragement that you have so kindly spoken to me
my entire life . . . I was always listening! I have benefited
not only from all that you have given me, but also from all
that you could not.
I love you both!

To you, the reader: It is my honor and privilege to help you
discover, create, and achieve your destiny!

ACKNOWLEDGMENTS

I would like to recognize and thank the following people for their support, encouragement, and belief in my dreams. I would also like to thank all of those listed here who have helped me with this book and my speaking career:

Kevin Allen, Robert Allen, Dave Beauchamp, Les Brown, Mike Bumpers, Corey Burkes, Bryan Caplovitz, Bettina Carey, Taylor Clark, Kathi Dunn, Brent Duskin, Bob Erdmann, Shannon Evans, Susan Friedmann, Rick Frommer, Mark Victor Hansen, Mary Heim, Michael Helgeson, TJ Hoisington, Matthew Holt, Dan Janal, Jerry Jenkins, Cindy Johnson, Charlie Jones, Paul Kadillak, Peter Knox, Jabez LeBret, Eric Lofholm, James Malinchak, Jeannine Mallory, Og Mandino, Jennifer Manlowe, Bill McCarrick, John McLelland, Albert Mensah, Art Mortell, Larry Olsen, Professor Jack Padgett, Jim Ploeger, Tim Polk, Dan Poynter, Anthony Robbins, Jean Schroeder, Shiloh Schroeder, Margaret Snow, Molly Snow, Tim Snow, Tom Snow, Christine Tew, Norm Thomson, Tyler Tichelaar, David Torres, Brian Tracy, Graham Van Dixhorn, Rob Van Pelt, Tobin Van Pelt, Shannon Vargo, Tony Wall, Jim and Barb Weems, Mary West, Mike West, Chris Widener, Zig Ziglar, and Beth Zipko.

CONTENTS

FOREWORD

When I began my career—uneducated, unskilled, and often unemployed, all I could get were jobs that involved labor—washing dishes, construction work, and even digging wells on farms and ranches.

Then I began to ask, "Why is it that some people are more successful than others?" This question changed my life. As I began to seek the answer; asking successful people for advice, reading countless books and articles, listening to audio programs, and attending seminars, the light began to go on for me.

What I discovered was that successful people think differently than ordinary people do. Successful people are more positive and optimistic, more forward-looking and constructive, more focused on their goals and objectives. Successful people accept complete responsibility for their lives. They never complain, never explain. If they're not happy with their life situation, they go to work to change it; they don't wait for someone else to come along and do it for them.

Successful people have clear, written goals, and every day, they follow systematic plans to achieve these goals. Successful people use their time well. They focus on their most valuable tasks, and discipline themselves to get started and to keep going. As a result, they're able to achieve five, even ten, times as much as the average person ever accomplishes.

In this powerful book by Patrick Snow, you'll learn all these strategies, methods, and techniques, and many, many more. A passionate and inspiring speaker, mentor, and publishing coach, Patrick has spent many years drinking at the well of knowledge and success, and has extracted and distilled some of the best and most practical ideas on leadership and achievement the universe has to offer.

In *Creating Your Own Destiny*, Patrick provides you with a practical and easy-to-follow blueprint that will enable you to accomplish more in the next year or two than most people are able to do in five or ten years, or even in an entire lifetime.

When you follow the formulas and strategies in this book, you'll discover how to leverage your talents and abilities and get more out of yourself and life. You'll learn how to decide exactly what you want, describe and write it down, and make plans for accomplishing that.

You will learn how to acquire the specific knowledge and skills needed to achieve any goal you set for yourself, your family, or your business. You'll learn what it takes to become a success— and you'll do it faster and easier than you ever thought possible, no matter where you are today or where you might have started.

Through this book, you will learn that you are the primary moving force in your life. You create your own reality with your thoughts and you have complete control over those thoughts. Let Patrick Snow show you how to jump on life's fast track and put your foot on the accelerator to your own potential.

So put up your tray table, fasten your seatbelt, and get ready for an exciting journey into the first and last frontier—your own mind. You may never be the same again!

Brian Tracy
CEO, Brian Tracy International
www.BrianTracy.com

Breaking Free

Your heart is born free;
have the courage to follow it.
—William Wallace[1]

As I have marketed and promoted this book, I have come to the realization that many people do not believe it is possible to create their own destiny. You will learn from reading this book I am *not* one of those people. I wrote this book to assist you in stretching your mind to consider what is possible in your life.

My goal is to offer strategies, resources, and tools to convince you that, despite the current adversities and obstacles in your life, you can indeed create your own destiny. Let's start this journey of self-exploration together by asking a few very important questions. Your answers to these questions will send you on a personal quest to seek the truth in your life, setting you free to pursue your destiny. Taking action on the answers to these questions will give you a life of happiness, freedom, and prosperity.

Are you *unhappy at work*? Do you want *more* out of life? Do you want to experience *true freedom*? Are you really *free*? Are you doing each and every day what your heart is calling you to do in both your professional and personal life?

I speak in front of thousands of people every year, and when I ask that question very few people raise their hands. Why? Most people aren't free. They've become slaves to their job or their life circumstances. They struggle with the things one "must" do: paying off credit card debt, working a full-time job (or even two jobs), taking evening classes, supporting their families and raising children, living from paycheck to paycheck, making monthly mortgage payments, and so on.

Even successful people aren't immune from believing they're "trapped." Most people I know who make a lot of money become slaves to that financial success. The more they make, the more they spend, and the more money they need to make. I come from a modest middle class family and I've achieved financial successes far greater than most people. At times, I have also severely struggled financially and not known where my next paycheck was coming from. My faith in God has helped me overcome many adversities. I have learned that money in and of itself doesn't make you free.

Over the course of a dozen years, I have interviewed thousands of disgruntled and unhappy employees across North America and learned that we all want the same thing: we all want *more* out of life. Most people basically want six things: more *time*, more *money*, more *freedom*, more *health*, more *love*, and more *happiness*. How then, can each of us get *more* out of life and recapture, as William Wallace said, our heart, "born free"?

I believe we become free when we create and then follow our *destinies*.

What is destiny? Webster's Dictionary defines the word as meaning *fate*. Look up *fate* in the dictionary and you'll see that it means *the supposed force that predetermines events*. I believe that this "supposed force" is your mind (or brain).

If we use our minds properly by taking action and executing our ideas and the opportunities presented to us in the way that we are capable of, then we truly can become the "supposed force" that predetermines the events that occur in our lives. To me, destiny means the ultimate purpose (fate) each of us has here on earth. Destiny is what each of us, as unique individuals, is put here on earth to do; to become. Our destinies reside within us. Destiny is our freedom, the great potential we have, the "supposed force" waiting only for our minds to unleash it.

By the end of this book, I believe that you will be able to discover your destiny. You will also learn how you can apply my ultimate Destiny Secret for life. This secret will show you how to achieve what the subtitle of this book promises:

> "How to Get Exactly What
> You Want Out of Life and Work."

I know what many of you may be saying: I can't influence my destiny. My job sucks. I'm worried about being laid off. My boss is an idiot. My credit card bills and student loans are too high. My credit score is too low. Or, I have to work two jobs just to pay my rent or mortgage—and I can't even *think* about saving for the down payment on a house like my parents owned while I was growing up. That's wrong thinking. Regardless of how bad your current circumstances are, you can influence your own destiny. You can shape it, make it real. I'm going to show you how in this book, *Creating Your Own Destiny*. Through this book, you will learn how to dream again. I will show you how to plan and execute to fulfill your dreams. As a result, you will soar for the rest of your life.

Still not certain? I don't blame you—believing we can influence our destiny requires huge thinking and an even bigger amount of belief. But each of us can think, right? Each of us can believe, right? Right. Each of us can positively influence our fates. As Robert Ringer stated in his book, *Million Dollar Habits*:

> "When your mind believes something
> to be true, it stimulates your senses to draw to you the things,
> people, and circumstances necessary to convert the
> mental image it houses into its physical reality."[2]

I believe this is how you create your own destiny. Your dreams can come true. As Earl Nightingale said:

> "You become what you think about."[3]

Another thing often holds people back in the pursuit of their dreams: fear. Following your dreams can be scary. You might be rejected. It will take hard work. There will be obstacles along the way. But you must risk pursuing your dreams to become free. You will learn a strategy to put your fears aside once and for all.

I'm going to encourage you to pursue the biggest dreams possible, the most (seemingly) impossible things. Why? I strongly believe what T.S. Eliot said:

> "Only those who will risk going too far can
> possibly find out how far they can go!"[4]

This book contains four sections and 16 chapters that will help you create and realize your destiny—I firmly believe it will allow you to have more *time*, more *money*, more *freedom*, more *health*, more *love*, and more *happiness*. I call these 16 chapter headings my Success Road Map.

This road map was developed to show you how to be courageous in your endeavors and proceed in the manner in which you are truly capable. There is a saying by Ralph Waldo Emerson:

> "Do not go where the path may lead.
> Go instead where there is no path and leave a trail."[5]

You can blaze a new trail. This book will be your compass and help guide you along the way.

Before we begin, I think it's important that you know that all the material here was developed through my life experience, which includes reading more than 1,000 self-help books, working more than 15 years in corporate sales, being a publishing coach, giving more than 1,500 speeches worldwide, and, most importantly, being a son, husband, and father.

Please know that this book is more than just my thoughts and suggestions. What you are holding right now is one of my dreams come true. I believe that my destiny is, among other things, to help people overcome their personal fears and adversities to "set their hearts free."

I also believe that there is no such thing as a completed education. Education is a lifelong process. In fact, I believe that I can learn as much from you as you can from me. There is so much yet for me to learn—this is one of the reasons I enjoy reading. I challenge you to become a lifelong learner and open your mind to the new ideas, strategies, and techniques offered in this book and many others.

I want to challenge you to think like a world champion. If you knew that under no circumstance could you fail, what would you want to do with the rest of your life?

I know what some of you may be thinking: Patrick, achieving dreams is easy for you. You're successful, have all this great experience, plus you have a wonderfully successful and supportive wife and two great kids. But I, on the other hand, am too young (or too old) and too broke and inexperienced to accomplish great things.

Whether you realize it or not, I am more like you than you might think. I have been a "struggling underdog" my entire life and only recently have experienced the realization of my vision. I am not there yet. I am a work in progress. I continue to fight like hell to achieve my goals. On the other hand, if you have already arrived, then there is no reason for you to continue reading this book. If you are like me and continue to experience adversity, then let's move forward together in pursuit of our destinies.

I sincerely believe that if I can work toward achieving my destiny, anyone can! Anyone—I repeat *anyone*—can influence and enhance their destiny. What's more, let me say this: I believe you have what it takes to influence your destiny. How do I know this? I was once in your shoes, feeling apprehensive about following my dreams.

Also, the fact that you're taking the time to read this material and apply the ideas and suggestions tells me that you have what it takes to reach your destiny. And finally, every negative can also be a positive. You may believe you are too young, or too old, but think about it this way: You have the benefit of a fresh start with each new day. You have your whole life ahead of you to accomplish great things. Now is the time to get started moving in the right direction.

I want to help you. I will be your coach along the way, your guide, your confidant. If I can do it, so can you. I believe in you. Think about what author, Nobel and Pulitzer Prize winner Pearl S. Buck said:

> "The young do not know enough to be prudent,
> and therefore they attempt the impossible,
> and achieve it generation after generation."[6]

Now consider this quote from Julius Caesar:

> "For lack of training, they lacked knowledge.
> For lack of knowledge, they lacked confidence.
> For lack of confidence, they lacked victory."[7]

In *Creating Your Own Destiny*, I am going to give you the training, knowledge, and confidence to win in your own game of life.

Finally, as you begin this book, consider the following words from Oliver Wendell Holmes. They reveal the tremendous power of our minds as we continuously grow:

> "Man's mind once stretched by a new idea,
> never regains its original dimensions."[8]

This book will help you uncover new ideas, get out of your box, expand your comfort zone, and help you pursue the things you love in life. Additionally, you will learn to overcome rejection and put aside your fears as you pursue a new direction in life. I wish you well on your new journey in pursuit of creating your own destiny. Are you ready to begin? Good—let's go!

Patrick Snow

SECTION ONE

DREAM

∽

The thing always happens that
you really believe in; and the belief
in a thing makes it happen.
—Frank Lloyd Wright[1]

CHAPTER 1

Visualizing Your Dreams

Tell everyone what you want to do and someone
will want to help you do it.
— W. Clement Stone[2]

People who are successful in all areas of life—in their faith,
family, business, sports—share a common trait: the ability to
look into the future and visualize exactly what they want to
accomplish. Here's what St. Augustine said about visualization:

"Faith is believing what you do not see.
The reward of faith is to see what we believe."[3]

Why is vision so important? Being able to visualize what it is
that you want to do or accomplish paints a mental picture in your
mind. Ever heard of the phrase, "Seeing is believing"? I'm sure you
have. When we can "see" something, even in our minds, we're
much more likely to make it happen. Another way to think of this is
by what author Alex Morrison once said:

"You must clearly see a thing in
your mind before you can do it."[4]

Let me tell you one way how visualization has changed my
life: I grew up the fourth of five kids in Owosso, Michigan, 90 miles
northwest of Detroit. My father was a teacher; my mother a nurse. I
was blessed with a loving childhood. I also was encouraged to
pursue any worthy goal that I wanted.

Well, at an early age I decided I wanted to play professional football! I can remember as a young child watching the Pittsburgh Steelers win multiple Super Bowls. I used to put my number-32 Franco Harris jersey on my black lab, Bear, and then practice my tackling techniques—although mostly what I did was chase Bear around our backyard in the snow!

I was always small for my age but that didn't stop me. I quickly began to live by former Alabama football coach Bear Bryant's words (which I still believe to this day):

"It's not the size of the dog in the fight
but the size of the fight in the dog."[5]

I went out for the football team in the fourth grade and was very lucky to receive some great coaching all the way through high school. Even though most of the time our high school had very average teams, my senior year I led the team in tackles, interceptions, and fumble recoveries; was named Most Valuable Player; and also was selected as first-team all-league linebacker.

Looking back on this time, I must say that this was no honorable feat since my senior year we sucked and finished 0–9. To make matters worse, on Halloween night in 1986, both our team and the opposing team had the same dismal record: winless at 0–8. Well, not only did we lose this game (named the "toilet bowl" by our few loyal fans), we lost in double overtime. Talk about a humbling experience. I learned that night that life is not fair and it never has been. I am sure that you can think of times in your life when you worked really hard for something and still fell short of your goal. The point is that we need to learn from our disappointments and move on by developing a "next" philosophy. In sales, I refer to it as, "Some will, some won't, so what, next."

My high school football earned me financial assistance to Albion College, a small Division III school in Southern Michigan, between Detroit and Chicago. It wasn't the University of Michigan or Notre Dame, but I was convinced that I could continue to develop my football abilities and eventually make it to the pros. I could see it in my mind, so I knew that it could happen. But something happened during my freshman year at Albion, something that would change the course of my life forever.

Before training camp, I was so eager to make a good impression on the coaches that I over-trained. Several of my rib heads would "slip out," that is, become dislocated from my spine. A trainer would easily pop them back in, so I continued to practice with the team for almost ten days. But things got worse as training camp progressed. We were practicing four times a day. At times I thought I couldn't breathe, the pain was so bad. Also, I couldn't raise my arms above my head. But I kept on, because football was my life.

And then, just like that, my football career was over. I finally listened to the team doctors who said that no amount of rehabilitation could prevent the injury from recurring. At first I was devastated. My dream since the fourth grade was gone, dissolved in an injury that couldn't be stopped from happening again and again.

Fortunately, I was taking a philosophy class. One of the assigned books in particular fascinated me: *Man's Search for Himself*, by Rollo May. The plot of this book, in a nutshell, is very similar to the William Wallace quote in this introduction: "We are all born free." However, if we don't act upon this freedom by cutting the psychological umbilical cord to our parents early in life, we will only go so far. To think of this another way, we'll be tied like a dog on a chain in the front yard, only being able to go as far as the length of the chain allows us.

Once I understood this concept, I knew that my career-ending football injury wasn't an ending at all—it was a beginning. I was free to go anywhere, to create a new vision for my life, to do new things. With the help of Rollo May, I learned that there were bigger things in life for me than the game of football.

My back injury gave me a chance to start over again; to pursue a new set of goals. Two of those goals were to become an inspirational speaker and published author while pursuing a career in the field of personal growth and development to help others succeed.

EXERCISE

Can you think of a time in your life that seemed to be an "ending"? What were your thoughts, feelings, and emotions at that time?

_____

_____

_____

_____

_____

Did this "ending" lead to a new beginning? What happened?

_____

_____

_____

_____

_____

Of the current challenges you face, are any of them disguised as an opportunity?

_____

_____

_____

_____

_____

A New Beginning

I knew that I had only decided on Albion College because of my dream to one day play professional football. Now that my college football career had ended, staying at Albion didn't make sense. I hadn't yet had time to think much about my future and what I wanted to do, but I knew that I loved the mountains and I wanted to explore the western part of the United States. So I sent an application to the University of Montana and was accepted.

On January 1, 1988, as an 18-year-old college freshman who didn't know a soul west of the Mississippi River, I jumped on a Greyhound bus with a $69 ticket to Montana. I didn't know exactly where I was going with my life, but I was confident that I was moving in the right direction.

And do you know what? Transferring to the University of Montana was the best thing that ever happened to me. I not only graduated with a degree in political science, but, more importantly, I met a wonderful woman named Cheryl Monaghan—who later, I'm lucky to say, became my wife!

We now have two boys, Samuel and Jacob, and established careers: Cheryl as a prosecuting attorney for King County in Seattle, and myself with my speaking, coaching, writing pursuits, and a life dedicated to helping others succeed.

Let me say this: regardless of how exciting it would have been to play professional football and maybe even win a Super Bowl ring, it could *never* equal the love I have for my family. My experience also has led me to be a firm believer that people must never set their sights on only one goal. It's too limiting. Instead, each of us should create a destiny that we're moving toward, a series of people and places as well as milestones that we want to accomplish in our lives.

Since I can't play in the NFL, I have a new goal: to own my own NFL franchise by age 50. How is that for visualizing a dream? I will have to raise close to $2 billion to achieve this vision, but I have roughly ten years to do so. I will be awarded an NFL expansion team. My team will be called the Hawaii Tiger Sharks and will play its home games in Honolulu starting by the fall of 2018. If I can't get a fan base in Hawaii, then my other plan is to purchase the Seattle Seahawks or start an expansion NFL team in Los Angeles. If you are interested in being a part of this NFL franchise and ownership group, I am currently accepting investment capital at the address listed on my web site. Depending on your thought process, you are either roaring with laughter, or buying into my vision. Either way, these are the kinds of visions that you must develop in your life. Your visions are invisible and possibly unrealistic to others, but they must become visible in your mind and heart so that you can transform the impossible into the probable.

I also have a goal to sell one million copies of this book. I don't know exactly *how* I am going to accomplish these goals, but I will write about the *how* later in this chapter.

After reading these last few paragraphs, you may be thinking that I have an ego the size of Texas. I can assure you that this is not the case. I believe there is a big difference between having a big ego and being self-confident! My parents raised me to believe that I can accomplish anything in life, *if* I work hard enough at it. My attitude of eternal optimism can be blamed on them. As a result of being raised this way, I do not believe I have a large ego, but I may have the highest level of self-confidence of anyone you have ever known! There is a big difference between these two character traits.

If *you* further developed your level of self-confidence and stretched your mind to believe in the power of your visions, what could you achieve in life? Your vision may not include becoming a best-selling author or owning an NFL team, but your vision is uniquely important to you and that is why you are such a special person. Focus on your uniqueness instead of allowing societal pressures to have you conform to becoming like everyone else. To set yourself free, you must develop faith in yourself and believe in your visions like never before.

The point about my new beginning is that if I did not have the ability to dream big and envision what my future could be, then I never would have had the courage to board that bus to Montana. Because I was able to see the invisible, I achieved the impossible—a wonderful family, a successful career, and an exciting future.

I challenge you to develop your own visualization skills and see your biggest dreams in your mind's eye. Later in this chapter, I will show you how to turn your dreams into a reality—but before you can do this, you must understand that visualization is the first step. When thinking of our futures, we need to learn to walk by faith, not by sight. Most people think vision is something that you exclusively do with your eyeballs. I believe that vision is also something you do with your heart.

EXERCISE

If you knew that you could not fail, what would your future look like? Dream big and fill in your visions below.

_____

_____

_____

_____

_____

_____

_____

_____

_____

A Personal Mission Statement

One way I've found to help visualize my ultimate destiny is to create a personal mission statement. What is a personal mission statement? In the 1990s it became fashionable for companies to apply for and receive ISO (International Organization for Standardization) certification. This is a process that a company would go through to document everything it did, with the idea being that organizations with sound processes and quality products and services could be identified. Part of the ISO process is for a company to create a mission statement: what do we as a company want to do, and what do we as a company stand for?

I suggest you create something similar. What it is that you want to do here on earth during your lifetime? What do you want to focus your efforts on? Be remembered for? Work toward?

On the following page is my personal mission statement written in July 1997. I've since modified it slightly. It will give you a sense of what your mission statement could look like. I have also included the mission statement for my business, the Snow Group, on page 12.

As you can see, a personal mission statement is really about who you are and what you believe in. To help you get started thinking about your own personal mission statement, think of these things:

- What do you want to be remembered for in life?

- What do you want your grandchildren to say, think, or believe about you?

- What do you believe in?

- Why do you work?

- What is your higher calling in life?

- What changes do you need to make?

- What are your visions?

- What are your dreams?

- What is your destiny?

MY PERSONAL MISSION STATEMENT

I dedicate myself from this day on to improve the world as much as possible by being:

- A strong individual who is a man of God.

- A loving, faithful, and supportive husband to my wife.

- A positive role model, strong influence, and best friend to my children—by teaching them values, discipline, respect, self-esteem, confidence, and love; as well as giving them the freedom to explore the world.

- A grown child who will make my parents proud, and someday reward them for their love and for helping to teach me how to become successful.

- A positive influence to those who aspire to grow on a personal and career basis—through my motivational speaking, coaching, web site, tapes, books, and other written materials.

- A positive influence to young people who are beginning to make decisions about their own futures.

- A successful business owner.

- A philanthropist actively seeking to help those in need.

- A happy, positive person with a good sense of humor.

- A caring and forgiving human being.

MY BUSINESS MISSION STATEMENT

The Snow Group

My vision as a business-ownership advocate is to help millions of people become successful in life by showing them how to overcome their fears, transform their passions into their own businesses, and ultimately create their own destinies! These "destiny students" will break free from their dependence on their jobs, and experience more time, money, freedom, health, love, and happiness in life as a result of becoming successful business owners. I will give back to those in need by donating my time, money, and energy to help the youth of today become the leaders of tomorrow!

Patrick Snow

AUTHOR

KEYNOTE SPEAKER

PUBLISHING COACH

ENTREPRENEUR

(800) 951-7721

www.CreateYourOwnDestiny.com

www.BestSellerPublishingCoaching.com

EXERCISE

Create your own personal mission statement. This may eventually take up one full sheet of paper.

My Personal Mission Statement

Name: _____ Date: _____

_____

_____

_____

_____

_____

_____

_____

_____

_____

Determine Your Destination in Advance

You must know what you want to accomplish before you can begin taking specific steps to make your dreams and destiny a reality. This reminds me of our last flight to Hawaii. My family and I boarded the airplane in Seattle bound for Honolulu. After the flight had been airborne for some time, the pilot made an announcement: "Ladies and gentlemen, I have two pieces of news for you. One of them is good and the other is not so good. The good news is that we have a 200-mile-per-hour tailwind, so we're making great time! The bad news is that we're hopelessly lost somewhere over the Pacific, and we have no idea where we are." The pilot tried to calm the passengers by adding, "We may not know where we're going, but we sure are getting there awfully fast."

Now in this case, we made it to Hawaii safely. But similar things happen to us all the time, don't they? Does your life feel at times like a lost plane, hurtling through the sky (life) "awfully fast" but also hopelessly lost? Many people are like this. Being able to visualize exactly what it is that you want to accomplish in life is a way to prevent this. Visualization gives your mind the ability to chart out your destination in advance (just as flight crews do every day).

Think about it: how is it that planes from all over the world are able to traverse across the largest ocean on earth and land on a tiny speck of land in Hawaii? There are many correct answers, but the best answer for this example is that the pilots of all these planes have predetermined their destination in advance. I believe that we are also programmed with the ability to predetermine our destinations in advance. We do this by creating a vision in our minds, then taking daily action toward this vision, and never giving up, despite what everyone else says we can or cannot accomplish.

I urge you to tap into your inner visions and determine your destination in advance. What is your vision for your life and where are you going? It is never too late to change or adjust your course— even if you are already in mid-flight. These mid-flight adjustments are part of the reality of flying. The same holds true in life. What midlife adjustments are needed in your life?

Visualization (the ability to see the invisible) is what allows you to live out your dreams and become fulfilled in life. A lack of visualization steers you down a course that leads to nowhere. It takes you to a place where you are not in control and resentment is sure to set in, because you've ended up somewhere you never wanted to go. This reminds me of one of my favorite quotes from Anthony Robbins:

> "The road to someday leads to a
> place called nowhere."[6]

I challenge you to take action now and live, *on a daily basis*, by the personal mission statement you've created. Note the emphasis. Anyone can create a mission statement and then do nothing to make it a reality—their vision never becomes real because no actions are taken. Successful people know that action—on a daily basis—must be taken in order to make your vision become a reality.

The ability to visualize your dreams will give you the confidence to pursue and fulfill your biggest goals in life. In fact, Toni Ann Robino, a friend and mentor of mine, has said:

> "When your dreams direct your life,
> your life reflects your dreams."[7]

Simply ask yourself what you wanted to become when you were a child? Once you recall this memory, then ask yourself if your heart still wants to achieve this goal. If so, dream big and pursue this passion with all your heart. If not, soul-search for your new beginning, then pursue your current passion with all your energy and don't let anyone's ignorance or negative attitude stop you short of seeing your light at the end of the tunnel.

SUMMARY

To conclude this chapter, I will now share with you how to accomplish your visions. I want to share with you the knowledge of a man who helped me take visualization to a higher level: I first met Larry Olsen about three months after the first edition of his book *Get a Vision and Live It* was published. Larry's expertise on vision has helped me answer the question of *how* we accomplish our visions. I am eternally grateful for his mentoring. Larry's book is a must-read, as it teaches you how to create a vision for yourself three years out and then live that vision now. My favorite words from Larry Olsen are as follows:

"I have no right to work on the 'how' until I can taste, touch, smell, feel, hear, emotionalize, and 'own the vision.' The vision comes first and then I see 'how' to accomplish my dreams."[8]

According to Larry, as soon as you own your vision, the "how" (in terms of how to turn your goals and dreams into a reality) will *always* appear.

For example, I had no idea *how* I was going to write this book, but the how presented itself slowly over time once I learned to own my vision and developed an unstoppable attitude. Similarly, today I have no idea how in the world I will become a football team owner or sell one million copies of this book, but as I learn to own these visions, the *how* will again present itself—just as it did with writing this book.

Most importantly, none of my visions will just happen for me, unless I first set them as goals. As a result of turning my dreams into goals, there is always a chance that my visions will come true. Without doing so, there is no chance at all. The same principle holds true with your dreams. *Someone* will attain your visions, why not you? Always remember this quote from Hillel:

"If I am not for myself, then who will be for me? And if I am only for myself, then what am I? And if not now, when?"[9]

What are your visions? I encourage you to think about your visions day and night. If you can do this, you will eventually take ownership of your visions and the *how* will magically appear. If you follow this strategy, then you are destined to get exactly what you want out of life.

It is my belief that if you are to achieve your visions, then you must do as W. Clement Stone says in his quote at the beginning of this chapter. You must communicate your visions with the world, and then sooner or later someone will show up in your life and show you the *how*.

CHAPTER 2

Setting Big Goals

There is a time when we must firmly choose the course
we will follow, or the endless drift of events will make the
decision for us.
—Herbert Prochnow[1]

In the first chapter we discussed vision and how to achieve your
dreams. We talked in big-picture terms; sweeping—even
grand—landscapes, very broad in nature. Now it's time to get
more specific. We do this by *setting* and *prioritizing* our goals.

> Definition: A goal is the progressive realization of a dream
> within a given time.

In other words, goals are specific elements of your big-
picture vision to accomplish or complete within a set time period.
If your destiny is a skyscraper, then goals are the bricks and steel
beams that serve as the building's foundation. Because this is the
case, it's imperative to understand that goals are the foundation to
realizing the destiny for which you were born. Your goals are the
key factors in determining the events that occur in your life.

The following is a John F. Kennedy quote on goals, which I
believe best drives this point home:

"Efforts and courage are not enough
without purpose and direction."[2]

Goals (which come from purpose and direction) are something that we can only create from our hearts. Many times, people get overwhelmed by the vastness of their biggest goals and question themselves by asking questions like: "Is my goal realistic or am I just dreaming?" "Should I listen to all those people telling me to just give up and settle for mediocrity?"

I believe that you should not just set your sights on your ultimate goal. It is far easier to just concentrate on your next challenge and then proceed toward your ultimate destination one step at a time. Otherwise, it is too easy to become overwhelmed by the overall goal and give up. Many years ago I wrote down this quote from Dr. Robert Anthony's book, *Beyond Positive Thinking: A No-Nonsense Formula for Getting the Results You Want*, that ties into this point very well:

> "Goals are not promises, but commitments.
> They are not wishes, but visions.
> And we do not dream and hope these dreams
> Are going to find us; we find them.
>
> Your goals don't start in your brain;
> They start in your heart."[3]

The beautiful thing about goals is that you have a choice: to build and create your own destiny, or to sit back, like Herbert Prochnow says, and let life's circumstances determine who you become and what you achieve in life. I believe that those who decide to sit back are like a leaf blown off a tree during a windstorm that flutters aimlessly until landing at an unknown destination. These folks end up falling to wherever it is that the wind blows them—beaten up and battered, eventually stomped on and crushed! I know this may sound harsh, but think about all the people in this world who have never done something significant and who then end up regretting later in life all that they would've, could've, and should've accomplished. Remember: "almost" only counts in horseshoes and hand grenades!

> ## A SPECIAL NOTE
>
> I was very lucky in my life that my father, Jack Snow, a retired high school science teacher and golf coach, introduced me to the concept of goals and having a written goal sheet when I was in the eighth grade. His comments must've hit home with me, because I've updated my goals every year since then! I'm eternally thankful for his guidance and support.

THE POWER OF GOALS

A person's goals define who that person will become and what that person stands for. Only those who set goals in sync with the visualization of their destiny will achieve their destiny. Simply put: your goals define you.

In order to establish your goals, of course, you must be clear on what it is that you want in life. W. L. Hunt once said:

"The first key to success is to decide exactly what it is
you want in life."[4]

Goals should have these attributes:

- They should be written down. Write down your goals, then keep them handy to review frequently.

- They should be specific. A goal such as the following is too vague: "I want to make more money." Instead, make your goals as specific as possible: "This year I want to generate $50,000 in my home-based business."

- They should have a built-in time frame, for measurement purposes. Again, avoid this: "I want to save enough for a down payment on a house." Instead, write your goal like this: "I want to save $x by December 31, 201x, for a down payment on a house."

- They should be reviewed and updated on a regular basis. Reviewing your goals frequently keeps them fresh in your mind. Plus, as events in your life change or as you reach certain goals, you'll want to update your master goal sheet. I keep my goals inside my daily planner. Other ideas include attaching them to a calendar, keeping them in an "important information" file, or in another location where you'll be sure to see them frequently.

Earl Nightingale was one of the forefathers of goal research. Here is what he said on the importance of goal-setting:

> "People with goals succeed because
> they know where they're going."[5]

At some point in your life (I'm hoping that point in your life is right now) you must search your soul for the answers to the questions that follow. I call these Life-Defining Questions.

You should take your time thinking about and then answering these questions. Don't rush through this. The quality of your thinking and answers will go a long way in the ultimate quality of your goals.

If you don't have enough room or you don't want to write your answers in this book, I encourage you to order my *Destiny Journal Workbook*, a comprehensive 30-day program to self-discovery. You can order this product from my web site. The workbook gives you plenty of room to write in all of your answers. You can also visit my web site www.CreateYourOwnDestiny. com, then click on "Free Stuff" to print all of the goal sheets to use time and time again.

Life-Defining Questions

Question 1: What are 10 things I want "to be"?

1. _____
2. _____
3. _____
4. _____
5. _____
6. _____
7. _____
8. _____
9. _____
10. _____

Question 2: What are 10 things that I want "to do"?

1. _____
2. _____
3. _____
4. _____
5. _____
6. _____
7. _____
8. _____
9. _____
10. _____

Question 3: What are 10 things that I want "to have"?

1. _____
2. _____
3. _____
4. _____
5. _____
6. _____
7. _____
8. _____
9. _____
10. _____

Question 4: Where are five places in the world that I want "to go"?

1. _____
2. _____
3. _____
4. _____
5. _____

Question 5: What are 12 five-year goals that will help me accomplish questions 1–4?

1. _____
2. _____
3. _____
4. _____
5. _____
6. _____

7. _____

8. _____

9. _____

10. _____

11. _____

12. _____

Question 6: What are 12 one-year goals that I must do to get me on my way?

1. _____

2. _____

3. _____

4. _____

5. _____

6. _____

7. _____

8. _____

9. _____

10. _____

11. _____

12. _____

Question 7: Where do I want to live? (Be specific: what state, area, region? What type of house? What do you want nearby—water? The ocean? Mountains?)

1. _____

2. _____

3. _____

Question 8: Who is the *one* person I want to make my journey with?

This will most likely be your spouse. As you read this, however, you may not know who this person is yet. But, if you desire to get married someday, simply write the word "spouse." Also, do you want to have children someday, and if so, how many?

The next thing to do in support of your one-year goals is to complete the monthly goals worksheet (see page 25). This sheet is designed to give you the ability to achieve your one-year goals. In order to do so, all you need to do is to complete four or five smaller goals, tasks, or projects each month that will lay the foundation for the success of your larger goals. Ask yourself, "Am I capable of doing just one thing per week?"

This monthly goal sheet can also be found on my web site under "Free Stuff."

On page 26, you will find my "50 Lifetime Accomplishments" goal sheet. This goal sheet is designed to force you to look at your entire future, then pick 40 to 50 things that you want to achieve. I encourage you to first list the 10 best accomplishments in your life to date. Then write what you still want to accomplish in numbers 11 to 50. You will be amazed by how focused you will become on your destiny as a result of completing this exercise.

WHERE TO LIVE

Some of you may be wondering about Question 7, deciding where you want to live. Let me explain why I believe this is so important to achieving your destiny.

Several years ago Marsha Sinetar wrote a book titled *Do What You Love, The Money Will Follow*. I agree with the basic premise as expressed in her book title, but I also believe people should take her philosophy a step further: live where you want and the money will

MONTHLY GOALS

January

_____
_____
_____
_____

February

_____
_____
_____
_____

March

_____
_____
_____
_____

April

_____
_____
_____
_____

May

_____
_____
_____
_____

June

_____
_____
_____
_____

July

_____
_____
_____
_____

August

_____
_____
_____
_____

September

_____
_____
_____
_____

October

_____
_____
_____
_____

November

_____
_____
_____
_____

December

_____
_____
_____
_____

50 LIFETIME ACCOMPLISHMENTS

1. _____
2. _____
3. _____
4. _____
5. _____
6. _____
7. _____
8. _____
9. _____
10. _____
11. _____
12. _____
13. _____
14. _____
15. _____
16. _____
17. _____
18. _____
19. _____
20. _____
21. _____
22. _____
23. _____
24. _____
25. _____

26. _____
27. _____
28. _____
29. _____
30. _____
31. _____
32. _____
33. _____
34. _____
35. _____
36. _____
37. _____
38. _____
39. _____
40. _____
41. _____
42. _____
43. _____
44. _____
45. _____
46. _____
47. _____
48. _____
49. _____
50. _____

follow. Once you have visualized your destiny, then finding a place to live that is compatible with both your goals and your destiny is imperative.

For example, I had my first interview out of college at a company located in Seattle, Washington, in December 1991. I can remember looking west across Puget Sound and envisioning how wonderful it would be to live on Bainbridge Island. I loved Seattle, and I loved living near the water, so to me Bainbridge Island represented the "perfect" place.

But it also supported my goals. The island is very close to downtown Seattle, with its abundance of shops and restaurants— plus access to the University of Washington and Seattle's professional sports teams. Yet the fact that the island is away from the hustle and bustle of the city provides me the time to think and contemplate, write books (such as the one you're holding), and otherwise escape and recharge my batteries. It is also a terrific place to raise a family as it has one of the best school districts in the state and there is virtually no crime.

Like most goals, though, living on Bainbridge Island took time and planning. When my wife Cheryl and I first moved to Seattle in 1991, we couldn't afford to buy a home on Bainbridge Island (or anywhere else, for that matter), so we found a place to rent about 20 miles northeast of downtown. But I continued to dream about living on Bainbridge Island. To help me visualize my dreams, we often went there on picnics, driving around, visiting the beaches and otherwise soaking up the atmosphere. We also saved our money. Five years went by. My wife graduated from law school and became a prosecuting attorney in Seattle. My sales career had stabilized and I was fortunate enough to be able to work from my home office.

In 1997, we bought a piece of land on Bainbridge Island to build our first home. However, qualifying for the home loan was not as easy as we had hoped. We were approved for a certain amount prior to having the home built. During the construction process, we ended up adding about $20,000 worth of upgrades. As a result, the loan officer was not thrilled because now the loan numbers did not balance out. We needed to show the bank some "contributing factors" in order to get approval for the home loan. With this being the case, I opened up my calendar book and showed her all of my goals (which were in the same format that is outlined in this chapter). As a result, she said, "now that I have seen your written goals—I can easily get your loan approved." One of the goals I showed her was to become a published author. As a result of having my goals written down, we were able to get our home loan approved because she could see that we did not pose a risk.

If you, too, had your goals written down, what would you ultimately get in your life?

We now live very happily on Bainbridge Island. Another of my dreams has come true. But, as you can see, this dream supports my destiny of speaking and inspiring others. Your goals and dreams must all interact—they must never conflict with each other.

Our next goal is to buy waterfront property on Bainbridge Island and build our dream home, fully equipped with a custom-designed lighthouse to reflect my love of the sea and passion for lighthouses. We already have our land picked out, and soon we will take action toward fulfillment of this goal.

Once this goal is attained, our plan is to purchase a Nordhavn yacht, keep it moored in Hawaii, and then spend our winters cruising the South Pacific Ocean with our family.

What does your dream home look like? Where will it be located? What part of the country? I challenge you to envision each and every little detail of this goal, then take action so that you can achieve your dream!

A GOAL COLLAGE

Here's an idea to help make your goals seem more real, and thus obtainable: create what I call a "goal collage." This is nothing more than a set of pictures that represent your various goals. Create this collage, then hang it in a prominent place, somewhere where you can see it often. Your office is an ideal spot for this.

A goal collage does two things: it provides a visual reminder of your goals, and, once a goal has been realized, it gives you a sense of satisfaction and a stronger belief that you can meet your other goals.

Please note that I'm *not* talking about something small: my goal collage is two feet high by three feet wide! Go wild, get crazy—create something fun and big and exciting that will help you get excited about your dreams (cork bulletin boards work great). Try a goal collage—you'll be pleased with the results. Make sure that your goal collage includes pictures of your dream home in the location that you desire to live.

SUMMARY

As I hope you see by now, having written goals is not a hindrance, a limiting factor, or something that you "have to do." No, goals provide freedom in that your destination has been set and you are now free to actively pursue exactly what it is that you want in life. Just remember to have fun at all times. As the saying goes: "Half the fun is getting there."

I promise that if you complete your own life-defining questions, then you will not only lead a more fulfilled life, but you will also be in control of your destiny. Your goals will give your life purpose and direction. Your character will never be questioned because everyone (especially you) will know where you are, and, more importantly, where you are going! Your goal collage then becomes a picture of what your future will look like in the place that you desire.

Finally, make certain not to create regret for yourself later in life. Don't die with your music still inside you! Set and prioritize your goals in a manner in which the world will hear you sing, feel your music, and ultimately, benefit from your efforts in one way or another.

CHAPTER 3

Putting Your Family Ahead of Work

Knowing who you work for—priceless!
—MasterCard commercial

Have you seen the MasterCard commercial where the father and son are at some exotic tropical island, swimming in crystal clear water? As you watch this scene the narrator says: "Knowing who you work for—priceless!" This is without question my favorite commercial. Why? That father has his priorities straight.

In the last chapter we talked a great deal about setting big goals. But there is more to life than the pursuit of achieving your goals. Money is important, but we'd also all agree that our children—and the children of the world—are far more important.

When all is said and done, very few people find themselves on their death beds wishing that they had spent more time away from their families at work. In fact, just the opposite is true. Most people wish that they had spent less time at work and more time with their family. From this day forward I challenge you to put your family ahead of work.

In doing so, you will learn the truth in one of my favorite quotations my mother gave me. This poem from Forest Witcraft is for all you parents out there who struggle financially for your family but still manage to meet your children's basic needs of food, shelter, and love:

A hundred years from now . . .

It will not matter

What my bank account was,

The sort of house that I lived in,

Or the kind of car I drove.

But the world may be better

Because I was important

In the life of a child![1]

The problem is that so many people today are working so hard at their jobs that they can't spend quality time with their children. This fact, combined with other difficult realities of working in today's economy, has led to an alarming increase in worker discontent and level of unhappiness. Are you one of the 50 percent of Americans whom *USA TODAY* reports are "unhappy at work?"[2]

While making sales calls over the course of a dozen years, I have tracked corporate layoffs and interviewed literally thousands of disgruntled employees. As a result, I have compiled the following list.

Overwhelmingly, the number one reason that I have found for worker discontent is their inability to get along with their bosses. Which of the following reasons contributes most to your level of unhappiness and discontent at work? Think about this—if you had your own business, would any of these apply?

As a business-ownership advocate, I hope that this chapter will convince you of the many benefits of starting your own business. To those of you already in business and who are struggling, I hope this message reinforces your decision to keep moving forward despite all the challenges that you are facing.

THE TOP 10 REASONS WHY YOUR JOB SUCKS!

10.   Not enough vacation time.

9.   No tax deductions as an employee.

8.   Unpaid overtime and working on weekends.

7.   Business travel away from your family.

6.   Your daily commute.

5.   No respect and no job security.

4.   Too little pay and no ownership.

3.   Worrying about being laid off.

2.   You work with a bunch of "stiffs."

1.   Your boss is an "idiot."

MY FAMILY

My wife's grandfather used to say:

> "Don't spend so much time making a living, that
> you fail to make a life."

He was right—but keeping your family financially secure can be a big challenge. It doesn't happen automatically, as you can see from my story.

I graduated from the University of Montana in June of 1991, three-and-a-half years after transferring from Albion College halfway through my freshman year because of my back injury.

One of my goals when I started college was that, no matter what, I would get my degree in four years. For those of you reading this book who are just starting college, or will be starting soon, I challenge you to do the same. Why? Because there are many benefits in doing so, such as:

- You will end up getting one to two more years of work experience than those on the "I'll-get-my-degree-in-six-years" plan.

- You'll save significantly on tuition ($10,000 and up).

- You could make $40,000 to $70,000 with your first job out of college.

- Combined, the two previous points give you a net positive cash flow of almost $50,000 or more.

- You can begin earlier getting on solid financial footing to buy a house or start a family.

How can you accomplish this goal, when most institutions today state that college is a five- or six-year plan? They obviously adhere to the *Tommy Boy* belief system—a six-year game plan to graduate from college (*Tommy Boy*, the movie starring Chris Farley, is one of my all-time favorite comedies). I suggest the following:

- Take a minimum of four to five classes each semester.

- Treat your studies like a job—put in eight to nine hours a day.

- Take all morning classes (between 8 AM and noon), then after lunch each day study in the library until 5 PM. This will free up your evenings and weekends to work or do whatever you like.

If you have already graduated from college, teach this strategy to your children—it could save you both a lot of time and money!

I am proud to say that I followed this course of action, and my family and I (and ultimately the people for whom I work) have benefited tremendously due to my graduating in four years. My wife and I were blessed with our first child, Sam, when I was 22 years old. Had it not been for my graduating in four years and already having a full-time job, I would have had an even more difficult time supporting our young family.

During my senior year at the University of Montana, I found a job doing marketing and advertising for the largest travel agency in Montana. I also spent a lot of time delivering tickets to their corporate accounts and changing the "day's specials" sign so passersby could see. I was treated like an errand boy by everyone except the general manager, Tom Schmidt, but I didn't let this get to me. Why? Because I knew that this position was only temporary—that I would soon be able to move onto something bigger and better.

My wife and I wanted to move to Seattle, so I began writing letters and sending resumes to companies in and around Seattle. Finally, I landed a job interview with a subsidiary of Holland America Cruise Line's marketing division (Gray Line Tours).

It was a cold and rainy Seattle day (imagine that) in December 1991 when I flew in for my interview. I landed that morning around 9 AM and had a return flight at 3:30 PM. I went downtown, had the interview, and was offered a temporary entry-level marketing position at $8 an hour, with no benefits. After six months my performance would be evaluated and only then would I be offered a full-time job (if my performance was satisfactory, of course). I wasn't thrilled with the offer, to say the least, but I accepted it because it was better than nothing.

So I walked outside in the cold Seattle rain. It was noon; I had three hours before my return flight. But I didn't go to the airport. I was, as motivational speaker Les Brown says, "hungry," and determined to find something better, so I scanned the Seattle skyline looking for the tallest skyscraper I could see. I spotted the Washington Mutual Tower building, drove there, then began on the top floor—the 54th—and went office to office handing out my resumes.

Most people quickly shoved me (figuratively speaking) back out the door, but I kept on because I was determined to find a better job offer. After more than an hour I finally landed in the office of Mutual Travel on the 18th floor. I walked in knowing something good was going to happen because I was already working for a travel agency. I told the receptionist that I didn't have an appointment but it was urgent that I speak with the vice president of sales because I knew that sales was my calling.

Well, to my surprise (and I think the receptionist's, too) out came the VP of sales, who told me that I had five minutes to tell my story. Five minutes! Well, thirty minutes later I was offered a position in the group department until the next sales position came open. The group department position was permanent, full-time, with benefits and a starting salary of $18,000 per year. I know this isn't a lot of money by today's standards, but in 1991 it was decent money. I wasn't Bill Gates, but I had certainly done better than the temporary job at Holland America.

In late December 1991, my wife and I moved to Seattle, and I began my new job with Mutual Travel. But I soon learned that $18,000 per year didn't go very far with a young family. After six months in the group department I was promoted to sales, but still was only making $22,000 per year.

To help our family, I took a second job delivering morning newspapers for the *Journal American*. It was pure hell throwing newspapers from 4:30 AM to 7:00 AM seven days a week just to make an extra $500 per month. However, I remembered who I worked for—my family—and I kept on.

The point of all this is that sometimes you have to do something difficult or tiring to help your family. But most of the time these difficulties are only temporary—better times and better opportunities do come.

While working two jobs, I also learned that not only is it important to try to maximize your income, but to also watch your spending habits as well. In the book *The Millionaire Next Door*, written by Thomas Stanley and William Danko, I learned that: "It doesn't matter how much money you make, but how much money you spend."[3] It's equally important, in other words, to lessen your expenses as it is to earn more money.

EXERCISE

Very quickly, think of and list 10 ways you can immediately begin spending less money.

1. _____

2. _____

3. _____

4. _____

5. _____

6. _____

7. _____

8. _____

9. _____

10. _____

MOVING UP

After nine months doing the paper route, I realized that what I needed was one better-paying job, not two lesser-paying jobs.

So I soon left Mutual Travel (and the paper route) to accept a sales position with Airborne Express. However, before I left Mutual Travel, because of my Japanese language skills, I had an opportunity to hand-deliver more than 1,000 airline tickets to Japanese foreign exchange students who were to visit the United States later that summer. Each ticket was valued at more than $1,000. At 23 years old I went to Tokyo (via business class) for five days, carrying a large duffle bag stuffed with more than one million dollars worth of airline tickets. Let me tell you, I was a bit nervous going through customs in Japan, and very thankful to get through without a hitch. It was a tremendous experience.

My new job with Airborne Express (now part of DHL) supplied me with a company car and an annual salary of around $30,000. It was a great learning experience, although my wife and I still weren't able to dig out of our financial challenges. Why? Well, as I quickly learned, the more money you make, the more you spend. Remember what Confucius said:

"When prosperity comes, do not use all of it."[4]

I strongly believe that people cannot pursue their destinies if they first do not have their financial lives in order. In Chapter 4 we will discuss creating multiple streams of income. It's also imperative to keep your spending habits in check. If you can successfully limit your spending, you'll be free (from a financial point of view) to pursue whatever your heart desires!

At Airborne I had the opportunity to relocate and go into sales management, but I refused because my family and I (again, the people I work for) wanted to stay in Seattle. Moving up into sales management would've meant transferring to somewhere like Spokane, Washington; Boise, Idaho; or Grand Rapids, Michigan.

These are all nice places to live, I'm sure—but we wanted to stay in Seattle. Plus, with my wife's Washington legal education, it simply didn't make sense to move out of state. This decision reminds me of John Atkinson's words:

"If you don't run your own life, somebody else will."[5]

After almost three years, I left Airborne and accepted a corporate sales position with Avis Rent-A-Car. Here's where I learned another important financial lesson: after I had worked there for almost two years, the company was acquired. I had little stock in their employee stock ownership plan (also called an ESOP). I had nothing, in fact, except my old pay stubs.

But the company had a lot—they had the million-dollar accounts that I had brought to Avis. Even today, the revenue from my work continues to flow into Avis. Talk about residual income—most large corporations have this wealth-creation principle mastered.

Through my next job hunt, I ended up at a printed circuit board manufacturer in high-tech sales. The lesson I learned was that if you don't already own your own business, you need to work somewhere that gives you the ability to become a part owner. After three years with two different circuit board companies, I learned of an opportunity to receive a small ownership position in the form of stock options with Merix Corporation, a publicly traded company on NASDAQ. This company had given me what my mentor's wealth-creation principles taught me I needed if I were to become wealthy: stock ownership. Because of my income diversity philosophy, I encourage anyone who is working at a job for income, but pursuing a dream on the side during evenings and weekends, to continue with their day job *until it gets in the way of those dreams.* What I mean by this is that, eventually through proper execution of your game plan, you will start to make the lion's share of your income from your own business. When this begins to happen (be it one year from now or ten years from now), you can begin the transition from a day job to your own business opportunity. Two other factors to consider before you make this transition are whether you have a year's worth of income saved, and if you are debt-free. I believe you need to have both of these things before you can make the switch.

From 1996 to 2001, during the early mornings, late evenings, and weekends, I wrote the first edition of this book while continuing to develop my speaking business on a part-time basis and working my day job full-time. By executing energy and focus toward my passions and true destiny in life, I have continued to realize my lifetime goals—even though my family and I have been through the financial ups and downs involved with pursuing this destiny.

Looking back, I can say with no regrets that all of our struggles were well worth the financial rewards that we have realized as a result of following my dreams. My faith in God ultimately gave me the strength to continue pushing forward at a time when all the odds were stacked against me!

Without question, you too will be financially and emotionally tested on your way to achieving your destiny. If your belief in your vision is strong enough, you too will overcome every obstacle that gets in your way.

Some of you reading this book may be questioning my loyalty—working for nine different companies over a period of 15 years. I see it this way: my loyalty and faithfulness belong to my family, not a company.

If you desire to get ahead in corporate America, you need to look for a new job, at a minimum, every two to three years, and each job transition should pay you at least 20 percent more than your current salary. How else do you think I went from making just under $20,000 a year to more than six figures in approximately ten years? If you don't look for and take new jobs this often, you will continue to receive the standard 5 percent raise each year at review time. If you desire to make six figures, one way to do this—other than to own your own company—is to change jobs frequently.

The time to look for a new job is when you don't need one. That's when you can be selective. If you wait until you have been laid off to begin looking, you will have far fewer options. You may, in fact, have to accept *less* money out of pure desperation.

One important thing to understand is that all companies are in business to make money (unless they're nonprofit organizations). Therefore, most companies are going to pay you only enough to keep you from quitting. Because of this, many companies don't understand why many of their employees only work hard enough to keep from getting fired. The only way to get paid what you're really worth is to own your own business.

Many times, it may take owning and learning from several businesses before you find your "pot of gold." I have learned many things from at least half a dozen business opportunities that I have owned over the years. I have taken these important lessons from each endeavor into the next opportunity, and have benefited from all of them in one way or another. Just because your old beater of a car failed on you at one time or another and left you stranded on the side of the road, you didn't give up on driving and spend the rest of your life walking. You got yourself another car and tried again. The same concept holds true with owning a business.

If you are content with your annual 5 percent raises, then all you are doing for yourself and your family is giving yourself the ability to order out for pizza one more time each pay period. That's it. There isn't much left over from a 5 percent pay raise after taxes. Based on the fact that you are reading this book, I know that you will not be content with only 5 percent and that you will demand more from yourself!

You need to understand that moving on to a new company is not an emotional decision (emotional decisions should only be made regarding love—who you will marry, etc.). All other decisions, especially career and financial decisions, should be based on facts and accurate thinking. Napoleon Hill understood this well when he said:

"The single greatest trait of successful people
is the process of accurate thinking."[6]

See, moving on to a new company or opportunity (including starting your own business) is a business decision based on facts. You can and will make new friends wherever you go, and your old friends will stick with you if they are truly good friends.

You may be asking yourself: how do I find a better job if I don't have the free time to pursue what I want? The answer is to let other people take you to these opportunities. Have others work for you to help you uncover these hidden opportunities. Get a recruiter of one kind or another to start working for you. Never pay the recruiter to do so (unless you are seeking your first job out of college). Almost all recruiters are paid by the company who is looking for qualified applicants. I have worked with recruiters on two occasions, and both times I was offered a job and accepted the position—both at a salary much higher than what I was previously making.

I have a tremendous amount of respect and gratitude to the large national recruiting company Management Recruiters International (MRI). Jim Kozich of MRI placed me in my most lucrative position to date in high-tech sales. Although I personally haven't used the Internet recruiting companies, such as www.hotjobs.yahoo.com, www.monster.com, or www.thing amajob.com; if I was looking to get a job, I would definitely check these out. Another option is to network with people in your industry as often as possible, as well as to regularly attend job fairs and job expos. Lastly, please make certain that you get someone to help you put together a winning resume (even if you have to pay for it).

If you are not interested in owning your own business (for whatever reason) and enjoy the excitement of corporate America, I simply urge you to make certain that the corporate ladder you are climbing is not leaning against the wrong wall!

THE CHALLENGES NEVER END

The problem with many working people today is that they believe that job security is attainable. Once they have a job, most people think their career challenges are over. This is false: job security no longer exists.

In today's high-tech world, companies face even greater challenges to remain competitive. These companies will do anything to build the bottom line, including laying off people. The funny thing is that they don't say that they are firing you, they say you are being laid off. For instance: you just happen to be one of the unfortunate ones. With the recession in late 2000 and 2001, I personally know hundreds of people who have been laid off, including myself.

Unfortunately, in September 2001, I too was a victim of corporate downsizing. Eight days after the September 11th tragedy (and after almost three years of a successful sales record), I was laid off by Merix. Thankfully, I received an attractive severance package and was able to get another sales position within two weeks with a competitor in the printed circuit board industry—TTM Technologies. This experience of being laid off was very difficult for me, but through this adversity, I learned the truth of what Nietzsche said:

"That which does not kill, strengthens."[7]

After 18 months at TTM Technologies, I was again laid off due to much of the U.S. printed circuit board manufacturing being shifted to offshore manufacturers in Asia. As a result of this experience (being laid off twice in as many years), I decided that I would never again put myself in a situation where I was dependent on a job to support my family. I remember driving that day, northbound on I-5 heading back toward Seattle, deciding I was going to transition my part-time business to full-time; and become unstoppable as I pursued my business goals. Since then, there have been many bumps in the road, but I have never looked back, and now my business is soaring.

It was at this time that I also launched my publishing coaching services with www.BestSellerPublishingCoaching.com. The publishing coaching portion of my business has been a great way for me to supplement my business as a speaker while simultaneously helping numerous people from all walks of life publish their books. As a result of these adversities and diversifying my business, today I am no longer dependent on corporate America to support my family.

I also created business opportunities for readers who ask if they can help me market this book. I created a Destiny Achievers Club, where anyone can create a part-time business and earn commission when booking me to speak. To learn more, visit my web site or call me at (800) 951-7721.

Getting back to layoffs, the problem is that when companies go through downsizing, the victims (including myself) have virtually nothing to show for their work except old pay stubs. Most simply look for another job, hoping that they can get hired (so that they can probably get slapped in the face again). This is foolish. Haven't these victims learned their lessons?

To combat this, I recommend that you do some soul-searching (as I have done) and turn your hobby into a home-based business. Then, if you do happen to get laid off, at least you have a second alternative to fall back on.

You owe it to yourself and your family to build something that becomes an asset, rather than just wasting time on a job renting out your skills.

After my experience of being laid off, I made a decision to build my own business in such a way that I will never again become dependent on a job to support my family. I have made a decision to become unstoppable, and as a result, my own business has sky-rocketed. At 36 years old, I retired from corporate America on my own terms, and now make more money than ever before in my business as an author, speaker, and coach. More importantly, I am now free and have complete control of my schedule and can maximize time with my family. If you truly want to create your own destiny, I encourage you to start your own business and do the same (but make certain you have a year's worth of income saved before you leave your job).

LEARNING TO FISH

My experience over time of getting laid off from two companies in 18 months taught me the true meaning of an old fish story that I am sure you have heard at one point or another. It goes like this: give a man a fish and he will eat for a day, but teach a man how to fish and he will eat for a lifetime.

See, having a job is just like getting a fish (your paycheck) given to you every other Friday. This is how you eat. When you get laid off and lose your paycheck, you starve! The key then, is to learn *how* to fish (how to earn money in a business you own). Then you can "fish" whenever and wherever you want, and eat as much as you want (earn as much as you desire), as often as you want.

I never really liked fishing as a kid because I rarely caught anything (even though I enjoyed all the time I spent with my dad listening to his stories). However, I absolutely love "fishing" for income as an adult because of the freedom it allows. If you want more freedom in life, you must learn how to fish for yourself.

There is absolutely nothing wrong with having a job because it allows you to eat. But make certain that while you are eating at the job, you work on your dream on the side and learn how to fish for yourself.

ENSLAVEMENT TO YOUR EMPLOYER

In talking about being able to provide for your family, or relying upon someone else (your employer) to provide your "fish," I'm reminded of this issue: are we really free, given this work-like-mad environment of the new millennium? At the beginning of this book, one of the questions I asked you was: are you free? The reason that I pose this question is that many people believe that slavery ended on January 1, 1863, when President Abraham Lincoln signed the Emancipation Proclamation. I believe that as long as we have jobs we are enslaved to our employers and are NOT truly free.

Given the fact that all workers are given a limited amount of income in return for working 50 weeks (out of 52 weeks per year) to earn their pay, it becomes obvious to me that employees are not as free as some may think.

If you disagree with this belief, let me pose to you a few questions. Why is it that employees must ask permission from their employers to go on an extended vacation, when business owners can go on vacation any time they desire (for as long as they want) without having to ask permission from anyone to do so?

The kind of slavery that existed in the 1800s in the United States has ended, largely due to the efforts of President Lincoln, but a different kind of enslavement exists today with our employers.

Some of you may be thinking that a six-month vacation is not really practical. Well then, how about on any given hot summer day: can you just take the day off from work and go to the beach together as a family? Or do you and your spouse need to ask permission from your employers to spend this day together as a family? As a business owner, you will be free and never again have to ask for permission to spend quality time with your family!

In talking about freedom and enslavement to an employer while giving speeches on this topic, I have been both ridiculed and admired at the same time. The ridicule has come from employees who still believe in job security and that their employer will take care of all of their financial needs in the future. However, at the same time, I have been admired and given an overwhelming stamp of approval from business owners because they flourish in their freedom and absolutely love spending extra time with their families.

A job is a good thing, but you must realize that it is nothing more than a temporary vehicle to pay your bills and support your family while you are building your dream. Being enslaved to an employer is acceptable only if you are building your long-term vehicle of business ownership in a field in which you have passion.

BUSINESS OPPORTUNITIES

When thinking about this controversial subject, always remember that 90 percent of the wealth is owned by only 10 percent of the people. The 10 percent are business owners; the remaining folks are employees. On which side of the equation do you want to find yourself?

The following exercises are designed to help you sort through your ideas and the various options that you are faced with in today's business environment. Remember, there are a million ways to make a million dollars—you just have to execute in one way. Follow your heart, and it will make the choice for you.

EXERCISE A

Sit quietly for at least ten minutes. Then write in the spaces that follow five business opportunities you've come up with (or have been exposed to) that can generate additional streams of income for your family. Think of hobbies that you could turn into businesses. Remember that a home-based business provides more tax benefits. Also, remember that whatever business you choose, it must be consistent with your values and goals:

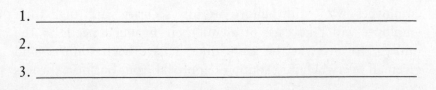

1. _____

2. _____

3. _____

4. _____

5. _____

EXERCISE B

If you don't feel that you can own or run a business, or have the desire to, then list some companies or organizations for which you would like to work (also list job titles). You should make certain that they are very stable and are capable of helping you attain your long-term goals:

1. _____

2. _____

3. _____

4. _____

5. _____

EXERCISE C

List five actions you can take immediately to help turn either of the two previous exercises into a reality:

1. _____

2. _____

3. _____

4. _____

5. _____

When starting a business, you need to align your passions with an opportunity that you can do from home. This will give you the ability to be there for you family. Shy away from any business that you must "lock and unlock" daily, unless this kind of business is your passion. Try to build a business where you can earn income without having employees, or not having to be there all of the time (you don't want to create a prison for yourself). I have worked from home now for over 13 years. I can't imagine going back to a daily commute. Because I work from home, I am better able to meet the needs of my family. If you worked from home, could you better meet your family's needs?

SUMMARY

Your boss is you and your family. This is a secret that most people never learn. One reason there are so many broken families is because too many people place more importance on their jobs than on their families. Your business card may read "ABC Company," but your heart should say, "My Family."

I know this sounds difficult. We are all challenged to try to make it financially while also being there for our families. It's difficult to balance both. Sometimes you'll fail. But when you do, you must try again. I believe that failure isn't final. Instead, failure teaches us lessons. And we all want to learn more, right? The more we fail, the more we learn. Henry Ford summed up this principle when he said:

> "Failure is only the opportunity to
> more intelligently begin again."[8]

In addition to Henry Ford, Thomas Edison failed on more than a few occasions. In fact, over the course of his life (1847–1931), Edison failed thousands of times while following his passion of inventing new things capable of changing the world. In 1879, he produced the first reliable, long-lasting source of light with his incandescent lightbulb. Here Edison is quoted regarding his view on using the knowledge learned from past failures to move forward:

"Unfortunately, many of life's failures are people who did not realize how close they were to success when they gave up. [. . .] If

I find 10,000 ways something won't work, I haven't failed. I am not discouraged, because every wrong attempt discarded is often a step forward."[9]

It's very important to understand this. If you still have difficulty with this concept, I suggest you read the book *Failing Forward*, by John C. Maxwell. It's a must read for understanding this concept.

As I stated earlier, no one ever ends up on their deathbed wishing that they had spent more time at the office, but many wish they had spent more time with their children, spouse, and loved ones. These are, after all, the people you truly work for—not the people at your place of employment!

I challenge you to spend twice as much time with your children, and half as much money. There is an old saying:

"Children are like banks. The more time you put in with them, the greater the return will be on your investment of time."

Also remember what Dr. Robert Brooks says about the importance of being there for our children:

"One of the most important factors that contributes to the resilience in children is the presence of at least one person in their lives who believes in them."[10]

Late psychologist Julius Segal said that this type of person is a "charismatic adult," a person from whom children "gather strength." I challenge you to be that person in someone's life in your community.

Remember that our children are, after all, the future of this world. If you don't really believe that it's important to spend a lot of time with your children, then please watch the movie *Traffic* starring Michael Douglas. His character, Bob Wakefield, almost lost his daughter to a life of drugs on the streets, because he was too busy and selfish building his career to spend quality time with her.

I challenge you never to forget for whom you really work—your family; especially your children, and yourself. Put your family ahead of your work and you will experience more love and more happiness in life.

As in the case of the MasterCard example used at the beginning of this chapter, I also know for whom I work. For this same reason, I am proud to say that the footprints that appeared in the sand on the early editions of this book's front cover are those of my children. This is just one photo from the many family vacations we have taken in Hawaii.

CHAPTER 4

Building Real Wealth

Surplus wealth is a sacred trust which its possessor
is bound to administer in his lifetime for the good
of the community.
—Andrew Carnegie[1]

In the last chapter we discussed the importance of putting family ahead of work. Many people have solid plans, but lack the financial wherewithal to accomplish them. They feel as though they need a tremendous amount of money before they can actually begin living their dreams.

Studies show that most people want more *time*, more *money*, more *freedom*, more *health*, more *love*, and more *happiness*.

Most young people today want a decent job so that they can save for the American dream of owning a home and having a car in the driveway. At the same time, most older people want to achieve financial security and someday be able to retire.

In this chapter, I will introduce principles and tools to show you how to get more money in your life *regardless of your age or current situation*. Additionally, if you play your cards right, more *money* will ultimately get you more *time* and more *freedom*. It is important to remember that money cannot buy you more *health*, more *love*, or more *happiness*.

Money is important. But too many people rely on gambling or lottery tickets because they believe this is the only way to get rich. This isn't true. Regardless of your financial circumstances, anything that you set out to accomplish is still within reach. It may take you working one or two jobs for a time, or having a part-time business. It may take a lot of work, in other words, but money is a necessary tool to create freedom. And freedom gives you the time to pursue your goals.

The key is to work smarter and negotiate more often. In this world, you either need to spend less than you make, or make more than you spend. Either way, you will spend much of your life negotiating for something or other, so always remember to ask for more than you want to ensure that you will get what you need. Too many people get hung up working at their jobs, living paycheck to paycheck, and they never make time to learn the principles of wealth creation and financial planning.

Your challenge then, is to get the "retirement thing" over with (i.e., invest enough money to retire) as early as possible, so that you can become free to pursue your destiny.

YOUR JOB IS A TEMPORARY VEHICLE

It's crucial to understand that a job is nothing more than a vehicle in which you position yourself to do two main things:

1. Provide right now for your family.

2. Learn, so that you can advance to the next level (whatever that might be).

Here's something I'm certain you don't often hear: I believe that work is overrated. That's right—I see work or a job as simply a method to support my family while I pursue my life goals. Having this philosophy about work will help you in many ways. The old concept of going to work for a good company to get job security no longer exists. Consider the following alarming statistics describing the high level of worker discontent:

- *ABC News* recently reported that ten million Americans are unemployed.[2]

- *USA TODAY* recently reported that 50 percent of American workers say they are "unhappy at work," and the numbers are as high as 66 percent in New England. My friends in Canada tell me that the percentage of people unhappy at work there is even higher.[3]

- *USA TODAY* also recently reported that 70 percent of workers don't think that there is a healthy balance between work and personal life.[4]

- The Gallup Organization shows 55 percent of employees are actively disengaged in their jobs—putting in their time, but with little or no energy or passion. They neither identify with their work nor promote company objectives. This results in loss of productivity in the U.S. economy at more than $350 billion per year.[5]

- CNN reported that in the year following 9/11 more than one million Americans were laid off from their jobs.[6]

- The Center for Creative Leadership reports that 40 percent of new hires end in termination.[7]

This is not a problem just in the United States. The same issues are a reality throughout most of the developed world. In fact, working conditions worldwide create far more concern than those in the United States. The information presented in the previous list proves that job security and worker satisfaction is a thing of the past.

Instead, if we are to make it financially today, we need to create "income security." What is income security? Income security can only be reached if you understand two main strategies about money and wealth, both of which I learned from one of my business mentors as a young man while in my twenties. These two key strategies are as follows:

1. How to get wealthy in today's business environment.

2. How to utilize four wealth creation principles.

Multiple Streams of Income

During my early days just out of college and working in corporate America, I soon realized that no matter how hard I worked on a job, my annual raises were minor—most in the 5 percent range. I also realized that if I was to accomplish the many goals that I had set out to achieve in life, I'd need to improve the vehicle (job) that I was driving. In other words, I would have to diversify by creating multiple streams of income.

Multiple streams of income is a simple concept: you have income coming in from more than one source. Ideally, the more income sources you have, the more money you'll receive. In the stock market and in the world of investing, it is considered common practice to have a diversified and well-balanced portfolio. Since this is the case, don't you think it would make sense to also have a diversified income stream? Just as it doesn't make sense to have all your money invested in one stock, it also doesn't make sense to have all your income come from one source.

Here are ways my family creates multiple streams of income:

Sources of Income

Keynote speaking fees

Publishing coaching fees

Sales of this book and audio CD

Sales of additional books, workbooks, and DVDs

Interest earned from investments

Real estate investments

Residual income from many home-based businesses

Spouse's salary

BUSINESS OWNERSHIP

Another common source of additional income is starting a home-based business. Many people also have tried network marketing and become quite successful. Network marketing (also referred to as direct sales or multilevel marketing) is a legitimate way to diversify your income and make money working from home without having to invest a lot of money to get started. According to the Direct Selling Association (DSA), 14 million Americans are currently involved in network marketing. Worldwide, many more millions of people have chosen this vehicle to earn money building their businesses from home. I know several people in network marketing who worked very hard and became multimillionaires from this industry, as well as others who have not worked at all and made almost nothing. As with anything else, you get out of network marketing what you put into it.

I have dabbled in network marketing numerous times in my career. However, I have always kept my book, speaking, and coaching as my primary business model. I have found network marketing to be a tremendous way to make extra income for my family. The beautiful thing about network marketing is that you can get started in it with very little investment up front, which contradicts other business models today. I will talk more about network marketing and direct sales income in Chapter 13, where I will also better introduce you to the Destiny Achievers Club.

If you want to work from home and own your own business, but you are completely confused as to what kind of business to start, then I recommend that you visit my web site, www.Create YourOwnDestiny.com. Click on "Free Stuff" to download and print a copy of "50 Home-Based Business Ideas (that you can start for less than $500)."

When getting into business for yourself, you must be absolutely certain that there is a need in the market for your company's product or service. This is one of the biggest keys to being successful in business, and a fair amount of research is needed to ensure success. There are not many folks selling Eight Track tapes or typewriters any longer—you get the point.

Whether it is a result of owning your own business or getting involved in network marketing, the goal remains the same—to build your business once, then get paid for life.

Imagine what it would feel like to wake up in the morning and know that whether you rolled out of bed, or just rolled over, all your bills that month would be paid. Financial freedom is a wonderful feeling. I believe business ownership is the best way to experience this feeling of more freedom in life.

A SPECIAL NOTE

All my extra activities are meant to produce income, of course, but they are also related to my life destiny and goals, which are to positively influence people through my inspirational speaking, writing, and coaching. Always attempt, as much as possible, to combine generating additional income with your life goals and ultimate destiny.

You can turn "if" into "when" once you start your own business in a field you are passionate about and sell your products and services to the public in volume. It is just that simple. This is the formula: executing your game plan on a daily basis is all you need to do to achieve financial prosperity through business ownership.

I know what some of you may be thinking—that you know of business owners who have started in business and are now stuck working 70 to 80 hours per week. They have no extra time and

IMAGINE WHAT THE RIGHT BUSINESS COULD DO FOR YOU

Imagine what it would feel like if you could take up to six months off each year and travel anywhere your heart desired without having to ask permission from your employer to do so.

Imagine what it would feel like if you owned the home of your dreams in a place that you always desired to live.

Imagine what it would feel like if you had a vacation home in addition to your dream home, which you and your family could enjoy for many generations to come.

Imagine what it would feel like if you had enough money that you could build your business out of choice instead of having to work at your job out of need.

Imagine what it would feel like if your children could go to college wherever they desired, instead of settling for a school you can afford.

Imagine what it would feel like if you could write a check each year for $100,000 or more and give it to your favorite charity.

Imagine what it would feel like if you could dedicate the rest of your life to helping others in need.

Imagine what it would feel like if you could experience the feeling of having more time, more money, more freedom, more health, more love, and more happiness in your life!

certainly no freedom. I agree that there are many business owners who find themselves trapped in this predicament. However, the types of businesses I endorse are those you can own and operate from the comforts of home. For this reason, I have been an advocate of home-based business ownership for years. I also believe that you will be better off to contract out some of your needs, as opposed to hiring direct employees.

I know what else you might be thinking: "I have tried business ownership in the past, but failed." The bottom line is this: all of us at one time or another have been left stranded at the side of the road with a car or truck that has broken down.

The reality is that we do not give up on automobiles and spend the rest of our lives walking everywhere just because we were once left stranded. Instead we just get a new vehicle. The same principle holds true with business ownership.

EXERCISE

Sit for several minutes thinking about ways you may be able to generate additional income in your life. List as many ideas as possible:

1. _____

2. _____

3. _____

4. _____

5. _____

6. _____

7. _____

8. _____

9. _____

10. _____

Now pick one. What steps can you take to begin to put this idea into action? What can you begin doing *now* to make this a reality?

A SPECIAL NOTE

Regardless of what you choose to pursue on the side, make certain that you do so without jeopardizing your day job's income stream. I have seen too many people get fired for working at their new business ventures while on the clock at their day jobs. You must keep these completely separate. It has been said that you work nine to five to make a living, but you work five to midnight to make a life. Lastly, make certain that whatever income opportunities you select, they are consistent with the following wealth creation principles.

WEALTH 101

According to an IRS publication titled *Personal Wealth*, in the early 1990s there was roughly $15 trillion in accumulated wealth in the United States. In a more recent study published by Merrill Lynch, personal wealth within the United States had climbed to more than $27 trillion. However, 90 percent of the wealth is owned by only 10 percent of the people. The question then must be: what knowledge does the wealthy 10 percent have that the other 90 percent are missing?

The answer is this: the wealthy 10 percent understand that the quickest way to wealth is through business ownership. They also know how to build income-producing assets (by building ownership and equity). Let's now explore each of these important concepts.

THE COMMON SENSE DEFINITION OF WEALTH

Wealth can be defined as:

> Owning income-producing assets that allow you to live in the manner that you desire, without having to work next week, next month, next year, or many years to come.

Wealth produced from these assets can support your family for many generations. Wealth, in other words, is a measure of the freedom it provides you—not your level of income. This is foreign to many Americans, who try to display wealth or give the perception of accumulated wealth through their high standards of living. Unfortunately, this leads to debt and a high consumption lifestyle that inhibits one's ability to create an income-producing asset.

WHAT IS AN INCOME-PRODUCING ASSET?

To put it simply, it is something that pays dividends. An income-producing asset is usually a financial investment that pays you dividends, such as stocks and mutual funds. Real estate or a business that you own are also considered income-producing assets. Having a rental property, for example, provides you with a monthly source of income. In many cases, a combination of all the above become solid income-producing assets. The goal here is to build an asset that will, for years to come, generate income for you and your family. For example, if you build a one-million-dollar asset over several years that pays 10 percent annually, you would receive $100,000 per year in dividends. If your lifestyle could be maintained on this amount, then you would be considered wealthy—even though you may not have millions of dollars in the bank—because you would have the choice whether or not to ever work again.

WEALTH CHARACTERISTICS

Most wealthy Americans own a business that sells products or services to the public in volume. They understand that distribution is the key, because volume requires reaching many people in many places. They partner with others to create wealth through mass distribution. This is vitally important to anyone who wants to be wealthy—the key to wealth is through ownership; not through a salary!

My oldest son once asked me how to make lots of money. I thought it was a pretty good question coming from a fourth grader—I could tell he was not content with his current allowance. I replied by saying, *"All you have to do is to own your own business and sell products and services to the world's consumers in volume."* He understood this right away—it's that simple.

One of my mentors uses Bill Gates as an example. Bill Gates did not become the wealthiest man in the world because he was the best software writer—rather, it was because he was the best in the world at selling software in volume.

OWNERSHIP AND EQUITY

You can achieve significant wealth by earning or purchasing stock ownership in one or more companies during the early stages of your life, then letting the stock or other ownership investments appreciate. In real estate, it's common knowledge to consider home ownership more beneficial than renting. If you agree with this statement, then why do you think so many Americans "rent" their skills on a job to an employer who doesn't provide stock options? A job, then, is really only renting, unless you build equity via stock options!

If you are working at a job (while building your dream on the side), make certain that you find an employer who allows you to earn stock options. With stock options, you now become a business owner. As a result, you will do a better job and ultimately earn more money in the long run.

HOW DO I BUILD AN INCOME-PRODUCING ASSET?

Four wealth creation principles I learned as a young man are as follows:

Principle 1: Business Ownership

97 percent of financially independent Americans own businesses, which gives them huge tax advantages.

Principle 2: Leverage Assets

Multiply your income potential through other people's efforts, time, talent, education, and leadership through selective partnerships. This allows you to, in effect, earn 1 percent of the efforts of 100 people rather than only 100 percent of your efforts.

Principle 3: Royalties and Residual Income

Expend effort once, and then receive residual income for years. A book or software program is a good example: a best-selling book can sell for years and years, yet the author only wrote the book once.

Principle 4: Take Advantage of Trends

Positioning yourself in the right situation at the right time can make the difference. How can you take advantage of up-and-coming trends?

Everything I have learned about wealth came directly from the wealth creation philosophy of one of my mentors. Because of this knowledge over the years, my family and I will benefit for a lifetime.

I also have learned another principle over the years that I believe should be added to the previous four:

Principle 5: Know and Trust Your Business Partners

Many people are like sharks, only in any venture for their own personal gain. Be careful with whom you do business. Over the years, I have discovered one way that works more than any other to determine the people you can trust—and the people you can't trust—it is simply by how people look at you. If while engaged in conversation people continually look away from you, they are either unsure of themselves or lying. Either way, you should avoid doing business with these types, unless you want to get burned down the road.

A SPECIAL NOTE

Two of the biggest drains on your finances are taxes and interest. It's mind-boggling to track how much these two financial enemies steal from your household budget. I challenge you to sit down sometime and add up all the money you spend over the course of a year on taxes (a good CPA can help minimize your tax burden) and interest (from credit cards, student loans, your mortgage, car loans, etc.). Once you have added this up, I encourage you to do two things to help minimize these enemies:

1. Start a home-based business, which will reduce your tax burden.

2. Borrow as little money as possible.

ANOTHER DEFINITION OF WEALTH

Wealth can also be defined as having an abundance of financial and emotional peace of mind. This can be attained by having more time, money, freedom, health, love, and happiness in your life.

Your best shot at achieving wealth is to combine working from home with business ownership in your area of interest.

KNOWING WHERE YOU ARE

As you probably already realize, keeping track of your financial life can be complicated and challenging. Here's one method that I've developed over the years to help me keep a handle on my finances, and it just may help you as well. This also has become a tremendous tool for me to ensure that all my bills get paid on time each month. (See the wealth creation blueprint on the next page.)

According to the book *The Millionaire Next Door*, written by Thomas Stanley and William Danko, your expected net worth should be as follows:

Expected net worth = your age $\times 0.1 \times$ *annual household income*.

I believe the wealth creation blueprint is a great way for you to see—all in one place—your investments, liabilities, and overall net worth. I update my blueprint every month. I also suggest that you list account numbers and phone numbers of the financial institutions for easy reference. I even use it to help pay bills—as a bill comes in, I log it. Once it's paid, I cross it off.

Consider creating your own wealth creation blueprint to help you keep track of your financial future. Once you have created it, it's very easy to update monthly. It's gratifying to watch your assets grow and your liabilities decrease!

Remember, building real wealth does not happen overnight. It can take several years to get to a point where you never need to worry about money again.

Another great book about wealth is *The Automatic Millionaire* by David Bach, who is also *The New York Times* best-selling author of *Smart Couples Finish Rich* and *Smart Women Finish Rich*.

SALES SUCCESS FORMULA

Studies show that there are two basic psychological reasons for people to make buying decisions: the *fear of loss* or the *hope of*

WEALTH-CREATION BLUEPRINT

Payment		Account #	Phone #	Balance
ASSETS (Investments)				
_____	House	_____	_____	_____
_____	Investments	_____	_____	_____
_____	Stock A	_____	_____	_____
_____	Stock B	_____	_____	_____
_____	And so on . . .	_____	_____	_____
_____	IRA	_____	_____	_____
_____	401(k)	_____	_____	_____
_____	etc.	_____	_____	_____
	Total:			_____
EXPENSES (Utilities)				
_____	Bill A	_____	_____	_____
_____	Bill B	_____	_____	_____
_____	Bill C	_____	_____	_____
_____	And so on . . .	_____	_____	_____
	Total:			_____
LIABILITIES (Loans)				
_____	Loan A	_____	_____	_____
_____	Loan B	_____	_____	_____
_____	Loan C	_____	_____	_____
_____	Loan D	_____	_____	_____
_____	And so on . . .	_____	_____	_____
	Total:			_____
	Net Worth = Total Investments – Total Loan Balances:			_____

gain. My sales success formula will help you achieve more sales now that you know why buying decisions are made.

Whether your background is in sales or not, as a new business owner, you must sell. Even if you have never sold before, you have sales experience, whether you realize it or not. How can I say this? Simple: Every day we all sell. We sell our spouse, significant other, parents, children, employer, and employees on what a valuable person we are in their lives. This is selling and it occurs on a daily basis.

How can we all become better at selling in our own business given today's competitive environment? After more than a dozen years in business-to-business corporate sales, I have slowly learned and further developed a formula for successful selling. This sales success formula has become my mantra.

Whether building a team, making a sale, or developing relationships, remember that trust (T), respect (R), need (N), and asking (A) are all required to achieve sales success ($). My equation is:

$$T + R + N + A = \$$$

How can we use this formula in all areas of our lives to achieve even higher levels of success (including making more sales for our businesses)? The answer is that people always love talking about themselves. The best salespeople in the world have figured this out and they try not to ever dominate conversations. The goal is to ask lots of questions, uncover customers' needs, and briefly explain how your business' products and services will meet their needs. Then it is absolutely necessary for you to shut up and let your prospects talk themselves into buying from you—while you are listening.

Listening is one of the most powerful tools in business, but unfortunately it is rarely used to its fullest potential. You can't learn when you are talking. The bottom line is this: friends buy from friends—people buy from those they like. If you want more sales, make more friends. It is that simple. The best way to do this is to talk less and listen more. Ask thoughtful questions to get to know your prospects better. As you do this, your prospects will grant you a deeper level of trust and respect. Then, if you can fill a need for them, you will earn their business in almost every occasion, if you ask for their business.

We need to speak 10 percent of the time and let our prospects talk 90 percent of the time. If you put my sales success formula to use in both your personal life as well as your business life, you will be amazed at how quickly you will attain a new level of wealth in both your relationships and your finances. As a result, you will get more *money* and more *love* in your life.

DOING WHAT YOU LOVE

Building wealth is the key to obtaining the three things most people want: more *time*, more *money*, and more *freedom*—the freedom you need to realize your destiny. I will discuss how to get more *health*, more *love*, and more *happiness* later in this book. In order for me to reach my destiny of helping others, for example, I will no doubt become more diversified and increase my wealth at the same time.

Many people overlook the importance of diversification. Remember that from an investment standpoint, at no time should you put all of your savings into one stock or one specific investment. With this in mind, why would you only have *one* source of income—your job?

When I ask this question, some have replied to me: "What would my employer think if he knew I had additional sources of income coming in?" My answer is this—don't tell your employer what you are doing in your home-based business.

Secondly, make certain that your own business does not interfere with your day job. Keep in mind that many presidents and CEOs are compensated one way or another by being on the board of directors of companies other than their own. I believe that they do this primarily (among other reasons) for income diversity—so should you.

Remember that your employer does not own you; he employs you because of your skills.

You must diversify—whether it means taking a second job, starting your own company, or opening a home-based business. Only then can you begin the path to true financial freedom and wealth, and move rapidly toward your destiny.

However, to put wealth in a different perspective, I do want to warn you to stay away from the trap of materialism (trying to keep up with the neighbors). This can be catastrophic over time. It was Socrates who said:

"He is richest who is content with the least."[8]

I challenge you to focus your energies each month on always improving your wealth creation blueprint. If you do this, your debts will slowly decrease and your assets will gradually increase. Over the years, through the proper execution of the wealth principles discussed in this chapter, your financial challenges will be minimized.

The key is to soul-search for your inner passions, then turn these passions into an opportunity or business that you can own. When you are doing what you love, you will never have to work another day for the rest of your life. This will free you up to more thoroughly pursue your destiny and, as a result, experience more *time*, more *money*, and more *freedom*.

Doing what you love (in the context of building wealth) reminds me of what two-time Race Across America (RAAM) winner, and self-proclaimed "million mile man" bicyclist Danny Chew said after winning this event:

"When you are doing something that you love, there is a seemingly endless flow of energy coming from within your heart that gives you the ability to accomplish anything that you desire."[9]

For Danny, this belief allowed him to win the RAAM on two separate occasions—riding 21 hours a day for eight straight days. If you, too, started doing what you love, what would your "seemingly endless flow of energy" allow you to accomplish?

SUMMARY

Breaking your dependence from your day job and building real wealth is not easy, as you will learn from my experiences. However, as you tap into your newfound energy, you are bound to start making more money as a result. Always remember the following lesson, which my father taught me well: just because you can afford to buy something, doesn't mean that you always should. The goal is to invest as much money as you can in an emergency fund or investment portfolio, so that you can attain a greater level of peace of mind.

The more toys you buy, the less money you have invested and working for you. This in turn means that you are earning less interest than you could if you learned how to spend less and save more.

Your personal finances and money are always at the center of building your wealth. If you like, you can view this as a game—a game that comes with serious consequences. Take the game of Monopoly, for example. When you run out of money, the game is over. The same principle holds true in real life.

Your challenge is to never run out of money! This can be hard to do if you are like me. I have invested a tremendous amount of time, money, and energy into building a business to create an income-producing asset.

As a result of having invested so much of my income and savings into my business and getting laid off on two separate occasions, I have come very close to running out of money and finding myself in a "game over" situation.

We have had our electricity, water, cable, home phone, business phone, and cell phones all turned off at one point or another. We almost had both of our automobiles repossessed. We also had been within a month or two of losing our family home that we built back in 1996. We ultimately sold our home and used the equity to pay off all of our debts. Since then we have purchased another home that we like much better. It is located on a golf course with a partial view of the water. We now have more equity than ever before and really enjoy our new home.

I am so thankful for my beautiful and supportive wife, Cheryl. Her salary as a prosecuting attorney kept our mortgage paid and put food on our table during these turbulent financial times. She was the saving grace that kept our family together given our challenging circumstances. I don't know if I could have made it through this adversity without her by my side. She is truly an amazing woman, a talented prosecutor, and a loving mother.

These times were *excruciatingly painful* for my family and me. While my wife, kids, parents, and friends all kept their belief in me, many others very close to me gave up and even encouraged me to quit following my own dreams of becoming a best-selling author and world-renowned professional speaker and just "get a job."

However, belief in my vision kept me fighting, and now I have built my business into an income-producing asset that pays me thousands of dollars per day for speaking, coaching, and doing seminars. As a result of building this asset, I will never again find myself in the dire financial straits I have been in at times over the years.

Through this process I have become free, since our family is no longer dependent on corporate America to support our needs.

Through this painful process of following my dreams, providing for my family, and trying to survive financially, I learned that nothing worthwhile in life comes without risk. I have learned that if you remain committed to your visions, take daily action in pursuit of your goals, nothing can stop you from achieving your destiny.

My challenge now for you is to do the same: follow your passions and build yourself an income-producing asset that will pay you and your family for life! The time is now and the best investment you can ever make is in yourself and your future. If you do this, you will build real wealth for your family.

If you are not content with your current level of income and desire more money, then visit my web site: www.CreateYourOwn Destiny.com. Next, click on "Biz Opportunity" or "Webucation" to see if either (or perhaps both) are of interest to you. I firmly believe both opportunities will help you achieve your destiny.

EXERCISE

What can you do right now to invest in yourself and start building real wealth for you and your family?

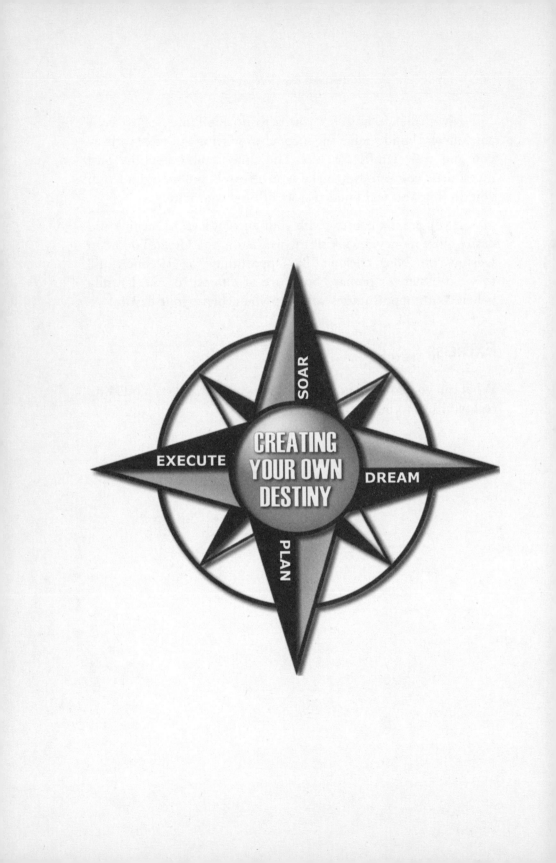

SECTION TWO

PLAN

❧

You will become as small as your
controlling desire; as great as
your dominant aspiration.
—James Allen, *As a Man Thinketh*[1]

CHAPTER 5

Creating Your Game Plan

The indispensable first step to getting the
things you want out of life is this:
decide what you want.
— Ben Stein[2]

By now I hope you're feeling better about your destiny—the positive things you can do and become in your life. You've created a mental picture of your destiny and also written down specific, attainable goals that support your vision.

But this next step is what, more often than not, stops people from being successful. Usually one of two things happens at this point:

1. With so much opportunity and excitement possible, people can't decide what to do first. They literally become "paralyzed with potential."

or

2. People rush full speed into one particular element of their destiny, spending a whirlwind of time, energy, and money in a "let's do this as fast as possible" mode. Like a runaway horse, though, this short burst of energy usually *looks* much more impressive than the *results* produced.

French filmmaker Jean Cocteau drives this point home:

"The speed of a runaway horse
counts for nothing."[3]

What is the answer? I believe it is to create a game plan (or blueprint) to follow to help you navigate along the path to success. If you were starting out driving on a cross-country trip, would you begin without a map? Of course not. Nor should you begin moving toward your goals and destiny without a similar course of action in mind.

Another way to think of this concept is this: many people who struggle with a sense of direction would not attempt a cross-country trip without some type of map and compass to help them reach their ultimate destination. As we discuss destiny (a derivative of *destination*) and goals, it is important to utilize any tool or tools that can help get you where you want to go.

A compass (a device for finding direction) can symbolize your goals. For example, if you determine that you want to travel north, then you will need a compass (goals) to tell you in which direction to travel. Without a compass (goals), you may want to travel north, but it will be extremely difficult to do so. Just as a compass was important for sailors crossing the ocean many years ago (and it's still invaluable today), so too are goals and a game plan important for your long journey to your destination.

Late U.S. President John F. Kennedy was the best example of someone setting a goal, taking ownership of a vision, and creating a game plan to accomplish this vision. In a speech before a joint session of Congress on May 25, 1961, President Kennedy announced the ambitious goal for the United States to send the first man to the moon and safely return him home. All of this was to be accomplished before the end of the 1960s. How's that for a vision?

This decision involved much consideration and an enormous amount of money and human effort to make project Apollo come to fruition in 1969. Shortly after the goal was announced, a tremendously ambitious game plan was created and executed over the course of eight years with the combined efforts of the federal government, NASA, and engineers and contractors from all over the United States.

Tragically, President Kennedy did not live to see the realization of his goal. He was assassinated in Dallas, Texas, on November 22, 1963. On July 20, 1969, Apollo 11 commander Neil Armstrong and astronaut Buzz Aldrin stepped off the lunar module and onto the moon's surface, as millions of people around the world tuned in on their radios and televisions to hear the following words: *"That's one small step for man, one giant leap for mankind."* Shortly thereafter, the Apollo 11 team safely returned home and President Kennedy's vision was realized.

The game plan that was put into place on May 25, 1961, has forever changed the boundaries of what is possible in space exploration. If you were also to create a game plan in pursuit of your passion, and take action on a daily basis, what could you ultimately achieve? This is a tough question, because if you are like most people, you may be thinking: "Okay, I have dreams that I want to accomplish, but I have no idea how to even get started."

If this is the case, it is extremely important to work smarter, and not harder, by maximizing the power of your calendar book or personal organizer, and incorporate the use of flexible planning to improve the daily habits in your life. Finally, if you do all of the above and fully utilize the goal sheets we discussed in the last chapter, you will become unstoppable and achieve what your game plan has put in place. Let's look at each component to creating a game plan.

WORK SMARTER, NOT HARDER

Famous architect Crawford Greenwald said:

> "Every minute you spend planning will
> save you three minutes in execution."[4]

I'm a firm believer in the old saying that "proper planning prevents poor performance." Have you ever wondered why the majority of people are either dead or broke by the age of 65? I think that one of the major reasons that so many people end up like this is due to poor organization, lack of planning, bad habits, and less-than-desirable time management. Most folks who fail in life don't plan on failing, they fail to plan! Studies have shown that many people spend more time planning their vacations than they do planning for their retirement.

I think no game plan is complete without the following three ways to work smarter rather than harder:

1. Incorporate a high-quality calendar book.

2. Use "flexible planning."

3. Develop habits that take control of your life.

THE CALENDAR BOOK

A calendar book is an important tool for helping you execute your short-term game plan and long-term destiny. You must, as the old saying goes, "Plan your work and work your plan." A good calendar book will help you do just that. Specifically, a calendar book allows you to list what you need to do to accomplish your goals, and also break these tasks down into daily duties and responsibilities. Only when you live day by day and accomplish small tasks will you create something monumental over the long term.

Here are some key elements to the best calendar books and how to use them to their maximum potential:

- It should be a comfortable size *for you*. This is something you will want to carry with you virtually everywhere you go. Because of this, you'll want something small and flexible. Avoid trendy products or those that are too big or bulky to be carried. Some, for example, can be more than two inches thick. I believe these are not convenient enough to be carried at all times.

- It should be large enough. You are going to want to include a great deal of information in your calendar book. Not only your daily appointments, of course, but also your long-term goals, your personal mission statement, and other destiny-related elements. Because of this, make certain that you purchase a calendar book that's large enough. I also like a large-sized format because I can comfortably glance at my calendar book when I'm driving. Again, find the size that works for you. I recommend a book approximately eight-by-ten-inches and less than one inch thick. I recommend the weekly calendar book from Letts of London. Most fine office supply stores carry these.

- Plan ahead. When you find a calendar book that's right for you, begin to look in October or November for the following year's edition. I find that I do a lot of planning for the coming year in December—you'll want the next year's book for this planning.

- Make certain that you only have one calendar, then record everything in it. I know this sounds pretty basic, but you'd be amazed at the people I've seen who keep a variety of personal organizers, wall calendars, and desktop calendars. I also strongly suggest you not rely only on a computer calendar. Why? You want something that's convenient, that you can take with you. Even laptops require charging and are not possible to use in some instances.

- Don't separate work and personal information. This ties in closely with the first point. Again, people who want to achieve large, far-reaching destinies have goals that support both their personal and professional lives. Use one calendar to keep these two areas tied closely together.

- Record your successes. Another good thing about a calendar book is that it can become a record of your accomplishments, a diary-like way for you to savor small triumphs. Recording and then later reviewing your successes is a sure way to increase your confidence. I have saved all of my calendar books, and I can look back and tell you exactly what I did on any given day since 1991 when I graduated from college.

SPECIAL NOTE: SMART PHONES

Today's powerful new electronic tools are called smart phones. I think these tools are incredible resources to help you better communicate while on the road and become even more organized.

These smart phones are a cell phone, a PDA (personal digital assistant), a digital camera, wireless e-mail, devices for watching movies and listening to music, and Web access all in one unit that fits in the palm of your hand. They can also be used as platforms for reading e-books.

Without question, the best smart phone on the market today is the Apple iPhone. This device can do all of the above and more.

Calendar books still have a place in your toolbox, because you can place photos of your family in your book, plus insert the goal sheets you created in the last chapter. This way, you will have these reminders with you wherever go. Always keep your smart phone and calendar book with you.

FLEXIBLE PLANNING

A second element to mastering time is implementing *flexible planning*. I first learned about flexible planning more than 15 years ago from Charlie "Tremendous" Jones. His book, *Life Is Tremendous*, introduced me to the concept of flexible planning. Without this knowledge, I know I would not be where I am today. To do flexible planning, I suggest the following:

- Throughout the month, consistently write down your deadlines, tasks, and responsibilities.

- Once you have all your "to do's" written down in your calendar book (not on loose paper or lists), prioritize each item in terms of its importance related to your daily successes. For example, you may have ten main items written down for a particular day. All may look very time consuming, even overwhelming. But by prioritizing the items from most (1) to least (10) important, you can focus on a particular task. You may not complete all ten items (or whatever number you have) that day. That's fine—the next day, reprioritize your "to do" list based on what is yet to be completed.

As a result of following this strategy, every day you will always make progress by getting the most important things done first. Here is a short example of what my daily planner looked like on this day:

MONDAY, JANUARY 19, 1998

1	⊗	6:00 AM	Aboard 5:30 AM Ferry (Bainbridge Island to Seattle–35 min.)
2	⊗	7:00 AM	Alaska Air #2700 (Lv. Seattle @ 7:50 AM, arrive Boise 10:05 AM)
3	⊗	8:00 AM	Read morning paper
4	⊗	9:00 AM	Check voice mail
5	⊗	10:00 AM	Call Dan (NW Customer Service Rep)
6	⊗	11:00 AM	MCMS appointment
7	○	12:00 PM	MCMS lunch
8	○	1:00 PM	Mail monthly bills
9	○	2:00 PM	Return phone calls
10	○	2:30 PM	Hewlett-Packard appointment
		and so on . . .	

You can develop your own system for checking off activities as they are completed. I recommend that you put a circle next to each activity, and then, rather than crossing out the entire activity once completed, put an "X" through the circle. This helps you when you need to refer back to previous dates—your activities won't all be crossed out and difficult to read.

A SPECIAL NOTE

You'll be, almost daily, removing and adding items to your main "to do" list. If you practice the concept of flexible planning on a daily basis, I guarantee you that you'll never miss another deadline. How many people can say that?

DAILY HABITS OF A WORLD CHAMPION

Habits are the things we do over and over. I'm a firm believer in programming myself to do certain things at set periods of time. If I plan correctly—again, there's that word "plan"—I'll be able to far surpass what I would otherwise be able to accomplish.

It's important to develop good habits in all areas of your life if you want to experience a tremendous amount of success. The neat thing about habits is that studies have shown that if you work on doing something for 21 straight days, then it becomes a habit and you no longer need to work to do it.

As an example, on the following page is my Daily Habits of a World Champion sheet. You'll notice that I created four main categories: family, faith, wealth, and health in an attempt to lead a balanced life. Feel free to use these categories or develop your own.

Executing your plan will be the difference between winning and losing.

Today's actions equal tomorrow's results. This requires world champion performers to provide leadership in all areas of life—by balancing family, faith, wealth, and health for the long term, while keeping a positive mental attitude that they desire their children to have when they grow up.

Family	*Faith*	*Wealth*	*Health*
Spend 2x time,1/2 $	Church on Sundays	Working 7:00 AM–6:00 PM	Premium fuel only
Saturday nights with Cheryl	Daily reflection	Quick follow-up	No food after 7:00 PM
Read boys 15 minutes	Teach children	Want vs. Need	No snacks with high fat
Many family vacations	Church activities	No wasting time	8 waters each day
15 minutes kitchen	Accept what can't change	Diversifi cation	Sleep 10:30 6:30
15 minutes laundry	Daily conversations	Project board	Walk 2 miles/day
Listen to needs	Copilot theory	Ownership without debt	Work out Tuesday, Thursday, Saturday
Protect family	Give of time	Save according to plan	Stretch twice daily

GOAL SHEET INSERTS

Remember all those goal sheets that you completed in Chapter 2? Well, here's another tip to successfully combine your goal sheets with your calendar: Simply affix your goal sheets to the inside cover of your calendar book (and first few pages if necessary). You can also combine these goals onto one goal sheet as provided on my web site: www.CreateYourOwnDestiny.com.

Now you can look at your goals on a regular basis—I strongly suggest *at least* several times a month. This continual reinforcement of your goals will sharpen your vision and help you as you prioritize your tasks and deadlines.

Another way to utilize your goal sheets is to check off, or highlight with a yellow marker, the goals you have accomplished. Again, this positive reinforcement will show you that you can accomplish worthy goals and will give you the momentum and confidence to achieve other goals. Momentum is important because as it builds, it can become almost impossible to stop—think of small waves that, over a period of time, become a tidal wave.

To further enhance your calendar book, here are some other things that you may want to add to the beginning pages in addition to your goal sheets:

- Your business mission statement
- Your personal mission statement
- Pictures of your family and loved ones
- Favorite motivational quotes
- Monthly goals
- Your goal collage
- Pictures of your dream home

Please note that it's extremely important to read your goal sheets often. Carrying them with you in your calendar book is an ideal way to help keep them handy. How many times have you found yourself with free time while on a plane, waiting in line, at the doctor's office, stuck in traffic, or on hold on the phone? With your goal sheets handy, even downtime can be turned into productive time.

Use your time wisely because you have a definite destination—the realization of your destiny. After all, French philosopher Michel de Montaigne said:

"No wind favors he who has no destined port."[5]

SUMMARY

Creating a game plan is essential if you are to ultimately achieve your goals and your destiny. Let me leave you with a story about how I used a game plan for success.

My wife and I ultimately bought some land on Bainbridge Island, then we built our first house. While it was quite an undertaking, we were able to create what we wanted from scratch. We lived in a beautiful custom-built 3,600-square-foot home. In addition to a host of wonderful features inside the house, we had a half-court basketball hoop in our garage that included:

- A 10-foot retractable rim with a fiberglass backboard

- A 16-foot-high ceiling and insulated walls

- Twelve recessed canned spotlights

- Two heating vents

- A regulation-size key and free-throw line painted on the floor

As you can imagine, it was a great place for my kids and I to play basketball whenever we wanted. The area was so long that, for years, my sons and I played catch with a baseball inside. Growing up, we never had a basketball hoop in our driveway, so I was determined to provide one for my children.

Did all this happen by chance? No, we had to plan, make decisions, and prioritize every step of the way. Our house and indoor basketball court was the result of many years of well-thought-out planning and execution.

In a sense, I created a small indoor gymnasium for my children. We played in there virtually every night all winter long and shared a tremendous amount of fun and laughter.

The result of creating and following a game plan is simple: for the first time in your life, you will have a positive impact on the direction you want your life to go.

If you remain persistent in this process over a period of several years, you will realize that you—not uncontrollable circumstances—hold the key to creating your own destiny. It's a wonderful feeling of freedom. I sincerely hope you experience it.

Once you have grasped this concept and incorporated this mentality into your daily life, then nothing in the world can stop you from attaining what it is in your life that you want.

Always remember that every winning game plan in life requires you to work smarter—not harder—while incorporating three separate (but equally important) elements:

1. Calendar Book/PDA (planning)

2. Flexible Planning (flexibility)

3. Habits (execution)

CHAPTER 6

Conquering Adversity, Temptation, and Addiction

My advantage is that I can endure more
pain than anyone else in the world.
—Steve Prefontaine[1]

To reach your life's destiny and to achieve more *love* and more *health*, you will need to eliminate all excuses and reasons not to do something. You'll also need to overcome addiction and adversity. One you can control (addictions), the other you often can't control (adversity). Additionally, you will need to gain control over your temptations. But if you are a person who can beat adversity, temptation, and addiction, and you also stay true to your core values and beliefs, then nothing will stop you.

Let me tell you about an experience that presented my family and me with a great deal of adversity—so much that we almost lost our lives. What's more, this adversity was the result of someone else's addiction.

On the evening of May 29, 1982, at 10:53 PM, my parents and one of my sisters were in their upstairs bedrooms sleeping. My parents had spent almost every free moment of the previous week preparing for my oldest sister Margaret's high school graduation party, which would take place the next day. My brother Tim, my cousin Tom, and I were downstairs watching a movie in the family room when all of a sudden, we heard the loud roar of a truck going way too fast and screaming around the corner of our street. Then we heard dirt and rocks scatter as the truck turned down the gravel road next to our house. Then—with no warning—we felt the house shudder as the truck hit it at an incredible speed.

I ran into the living room. The truck had smashed into the foundation of our house and in doing so, had pushed our gas meter into our basement's foundation. Every window on the west side of the house was engulfed in bright orange flames. I ran out of the house screaming, "Fire! Fire!" and everyone followed out the front door.

A neighbor across the street had witnessed the accident and called the fire department. Our family stood outside and watched our house burn. The truck driver—who, it turned out later, was driving drunk—had slammed his truck directly into the side of our house at about 40 mph and had hit our gas meter dead on. The heat from the engine and the crash ignited the natural gas line, which had broken upon impact.

Although the fire department and police arrived quickly, the gas line was buried beneath the road so the fire department couldn't turn off the gas. Our house burned until 12:30 AM. One side of our two-story home was destroyed.

During this time, my family, along with about 50 other curious people, stood watching the fire in shock and horror. The driver of the truck, who at first ran away and returned only after my cousin chased him down, stood in the yard screaming at my mother, "Save my truck! Save my truck!" Being drunk, he actually put his arm around my mother's shoulder—she was standing there in her nightgown—and started shaking her! I stepped between them just as the officer grabbed this man to escort him to the police car. To this day I can vividly remember the drunken stench from the man and the intense heat of the fire.

When the fire was finally put out, we stood huddled in our yard together. I'll never forget my mother's words:

"Everything will be fine, because no one died
and we're all safely together."

Now realize that when my mother, Lois Snow, said this, we:

- Did not have a place to sleep

- Did not have any clothes or personal items

- Did not have any food

The fire and smoke had ruined everything, but my mother was fine. Sure, she was shaken, just like we all were; but she didn't focus on the adversity we had faced or would face in the weeks and months ahead. Instead, she focused on the fact that we were all safe and alive! I strongly believe that my character was forever changed by that moment. Today, my tendency to always be optimistic in life was greatly influenced by my mother that day, by her ability to see our cup as "half-full," not "half-empty."

Needless to say, having a major house fire is not a one-day problem. That night we slept on the floor of the church across the street. The next morning we returned to our home. The fire marshal investigating the accident told us that we were all lucky to be alive. The gas meter, he explained, had been pushed into the basement wall, but thankfully there had been a small gap to allow the gas to escape. Had the meter been pushed into the basement an additional half inch, the house would have immediately exploded into a ball of fire and we would have all, more than likely, perished.

We *were* lucky to be alive! My family got a second chance at life. I believe, with each passing day, all of us get a "second chance" because tomorrows are not promised (as we learned from the tragedies of September 11). The question that I want to pose to you is this: what are you going to do each day with your second chance on life?

LIFE LESSONS

All of us will face adversity. It's part of life. The adversity may not be as scary as having a house fire, or being a family victim of the September 11 tragedies, but the challenges along the road to your destiny can be just as severe. Watching my parents deal with, and overcome, the adversity of our house fire showed me the importance of a positive attitude.

My mother didn't focus or dwell on what had happened—the negative; she focused on the positive. This strength of character served her again years later, when she successfully battled and overcame breast cancer.

EXERCISE

Think of a time when you faced a serious physical adversity, such as an accident or major illness.

What fears did you face at the time?

_____

_____

_____

_____

What factors helped you overcome this adversity?

_____

_____

_____

_____

What lessons or beliefs did this adversity bring forth that you still use today?

_____

_____

Overcoming Adversity

Here are some specific ways to both anticipate adversities and to overcome them when they do enter your life.

- Understand that adversities are only temporary (better times are bound to come). Nothing lasts forever, in other words. Focus as much as possible on solutions rather than the negative aspects of the adversity.

- Appreciate all that is good in your life. Even when something bad happens, you still have many positive things to draw on: your health, family, children, freedom, and so forth.

- Remember the people before you who have persevered when faced with more difficult times: Holocaust survivors, victims of war, POWs, and so forth.

- Know deep in your heart that you have what it takes to persevere. You can face and overcome adversities. You've done it before, you'll do it again.

- Understand that when one door closes, another almost always opens up. Look for hidden opportunities when faced with an adversity; something positive is almost always lurking close behind.

Dealing with Temptation

As we slowly overcome adversity, we often fall victim to our own temptations. Then, once we bow to temptation, it gets the better of us and we start making the same mistakes over and over again. If we fall into this trap, life's temptations can literally steal years of time away from our already short lives. This reality reminds me of David Norris' words on time:

"How you spend your time is more important
than how you spend your money.
Money mistakes can be corrected,
but time is gone forever."[2]

I found a powerful Native American story that I believe best describes how our minds work with regards to temptation—what follows is the legend of "Two Wolves":

An old Cherokee is teaching his grandson about life.

"A fight is going on inside me," he said to the boy. "It is a terrible fight and it is between two wolves. One is evil—he is anger, envy, sorrow, regret, greed, arrogance, self-pity, guilt, resentment, inferiority, lies, false pride, superiority, and ego." He continued, "The other is good—he is joy, peace, love, hope, serenity, humility, kindness, benevolence, empathy, generosity, truth, compassion and faith.

This same fight is going on inside you, and inside every other person, too."

The grandson thought about it for a minute and then asked his grandfather, "Which wolf will win?"

The old Cherokee simply replied, "The one you feed."[3]

I challenge you to feed only the good wolf. If you do so, you will be able to overcome adversity, temptation, and addictions. As a result, your mind will be free to follow your heart and create your own destiny in life.

The Horror of Addictions

Having our home burn was an adversity my entire family had to overcome. But closely linked to why our house burned was the reason—a drunken driver.

I was 13 years old when this event happened. While 13 is relatively young, I was still able to see what alcohol abuse can do to a society in general and individuals in particular. That night, May 29, 1982, I committed myself to a principle that I am proud to say I've always lived by: never ever get drunk. In fact, I refuse to drink alcohol, period.

I saw firsthand what alcohol can do. I've seen in others the fear that develops when alcohol takes control of their lives. Because of this experience, I am proud to state that I am a man of my word and principles—to this day I still do not drink.

Don't get me wrong: I don't believe that drinking alcohol is wrong. However, I am certain that drinking and driving is dead wrong. But for me, I choose not to drink. My friends and others have sometimes made fun of me for this, but I'm okay with it, because no amount of ridicule will ever change my core principles.

Remember this advice:

> "If you don't stand for something,
> you'll fall for anything!"

What your addiction is doesn't matter: it may be alcohol, nicotine, overeating, drugs, pornography, or a hundred other things that, when abused, can harm you and others. If not conquered, these addictions will take control of you. They will beat you down and they will stop you from reaching your destiny. In fact, Epictetus said:

> "No man is free who is not a master of himself."[4]

EXERCISE

What addictions (or similar bad habits) are in your life that you'd like to stop doing?

_____

_____

_____

_____

Up to this point, what has stopped you from stopping?

_____

_____

_____

_____

What steps can you begin to take *today* to stop your addiction or bad habit?

_____

_____

_____

_____

Overconsumption of alcohol and other substances are bad for your health. To paraphrase motivational speaker and author Zig

Ziglar: if you owned a million-dollar race horse, you wouldn't let it stay up nights boozin', smoking, and drinking coffee like there's no tomorrow, would you? Absolutely not. So why would we treat our own bodies this way?

How to Conquer Addictions

I know—it's easy to *say* don't do something, but actually *not doing* it is much harder. I realize that. Here are some suggestions that you may want to utilize to help you conquer your addictions.

- Acknowledge the fact that you have a problem. Often this is a relief to people. They don't have to hide or pretend any longer.

- Ask yourself this question: what will likely happen to me if I don't conquer this addiction over time? Will you damage your health? Could you possibly be charged with a crime? Would it cause embarrassment or other problems for your family? Could you lose your job?

- Seek professional help. Everyone needs help at some point, especially dealing with a long-held habit or addiction.

- Join a support group such as Debtors Anonymous, Overeaters Anonymous, Alcoholics Anonymous, and so forth.

- Live one day at a time. Don't expect to be perfect from the outset. Just as a habit or an addiction took hold over time, it will take a certain amount of time to stop.

- Focus daily on your long-term goals. Again, this will help you focus on something positive in your life—a point in the future that you can move toward.

As a result of conquering your addictions, you will ultimately get two things that most everyone wants—more *health* and more *love*.

THE POWER OF A POSITIVE ATTITUDE

Many people have asked me a variation on this question: "Patrick, I'm struggling to conquer my addictions and adversities, but it's difficult to do so and keep a positive attitude. How do I stay positive during these difficult times?"

That's a good question. It's also an important one, because only those who can conquer adversity and overcome addictions will achieve their destinies. One thing I suggest is to try never to get discouraged. You will face challenges—that's part of life—but don't let them beat you. Instead, focus on the big picture, on the many things that you have to be thankful for. Franklin Delano Roosevelt said:

> "When you come to the end of your rope,
> tie a knot and hang on."[5]

Here's an example of someone who always focused on what's positive in his life. Several years ago, when I was making a sales call on Intel, I met a patriotic veteran named Ron Dyer. He had two small American flags in his office as a show of his patriotism. I asked Ron to share with me some of his life philosophies. He said that because he'd had multiple tours of duty in Vietnam and that his life had been at stake dozens of times, he was able to keep things in perspective. Ron Dyer then said:

> "Every day that goes by in which I am not shot at
> is a good day, regardless of what else happens to me."[6]

How's that for a life philosophy? I think this is a good quote for all of us, to learn how to overcome the many daily adversities we all face—to keep our problems in perspective. When life gets you down, focus instead on what you have; what you can be grateful for. I challenge you to start each day mentally reviewing all the positive things in your life. Don't celebrate Thanksgiving only once a year. Why not count your blessings every day?

If you are still challenged to find the good in life and acknowledge all that you are blessed with, I encourage you to read the following poem. It is filled with statistics on how good we really have it in life. If these statistics are even halfway true, then we have little, if anything, to be depressed about.

BLESSINGS
Stephen Eardley

If you woke up this morning with more health than illness, you are more blessed than the million who won't survive the week.

If you have never experienced the danger of battle, the loneliness of imprisonment, and agony of torture, or the pangs of starvation, you are ahead of 20 million people around the world.

If you can attend a church meeting without fear of harassment, arrest, torture, or death, you are more blessed than almost three billion people in the world.

If you have food in your refrigerator, clothes on your back, a roof over your head and a place to sleep, you are richer than 75% of this world.

If you have money in the bank, in your wallet, and spare change in a dish someplace, you are among the top 8% of the world's wealthy.

If you can hold up your head with a smile on your face and are truly thankful, you are blessed because the majority can, but most do not.

If you can read this message, you are more blessed than over two billion people in the world that cannot read anything at all.

You are so blessed in ways you may never even know.[7]

EXERCISE

Spend a few minutes thinking about all that you have to be thankful for, then list as many as you can in the space provided. Refer to this page later when you're feeling particularly down.

_____

_____

_____

_____

_____

Now write out all the things in your life that you are grateful for that you may lose if you do not overcome your addictions:

_____

_____

_____

_____

_____

SUMMARY

There's no question that you will face many adversities in life, both large and small. You may also have addictions or other bad habits that are holding you back from reaching your goals. Occasionally, we will all give in to one sort of temptation or another. But only the people who are prepared to face and then overcome adversity, temptation, and addiction will reach their fullest potential.

Always try to think of what the future holds for you—you need to take responsibility for your actions. Never underestimate how wonderful and blessed you are to be in good health. You have a lot of things in life to be grateful for—don't take anything for granted.

If you want more *health* in your life, my challenge to you is this: don't let adversity, temptation, addiction, or making a living rob you of your health. Health is always more important than money—just ask people who have lost their health but still have money.

When faced with a challenge, refer back to this chapter. Don't get caught up in self-pity; you can and will overcome anything that life presents to you. As you overcome these challenges, you will certainly experience more *health* and more *love* as a result.

CHAPTER 7

Overcoming Your Fears

There is no impossibility to him who stands prepared to conquer every hazard. The fearful are failing.
—Sarah J. Hale[1]

In the last several chapters, we've talked about creating a firm financial footing; putting family ahead of work; and conquering adversity, temptation, and addiction. Now is the time to begin implementing your next steps and go. In other words, let the fun begin.

This also is the point where many people falter. Why? The planning and preparing are behind them. They must take action. Taking action can be—to many people—scary. Their fears are often so strong and compelling that their actions are ineffective—*if* they take any action at all. Author David Joseph Schwartz said:

"Do what you fear and the fear disappears."[2]

I use several sayings to help me remember the importance of taking action, all of which help me overcome fear:

"Taking action overcomes your fears."[3]

"Action equals results."[4]

"Massive action equals massive results."[5]

"This year's efforts pay next year's bills."[6]

"Today's work will fund tomorrow's
biggest dreams."[7]

Author and speaker Les Brown tells us that:

"You are currently molding your future; whatever you are now
doing will result in what your future holds for you."[8]

I believe that what Les Brown says about taking action is one
of the ultimate truths in life. Here's another way to look at the
concept of taking action: I have saved the following excerpt from
Murray McBride's forum for many years because I believe it
emphasizes how important taking action is, especially when put
in the context of fear:

"Every morning in Africa, a gazelle wakes up.
It knows it must out-run the fastest lion or it will be killed.

Every morning in Africa, a lion wakes up.
It knows it must out-run the slowest gazelle or it will starve.

It doesn't matter whether you're a lion or a gazelle:
when the sun comes up, you'd better be running!"[9]

EXERCISE

Think back to a time when you were ready to make a big decision,
such as starting your own business or moving to a new city.

Did fear arise?

_____

_____

_____

_____

How so?

_____

_____

_____

_____

_____

What did you do to lessen and, eventually, overcome this fear?

_____

_____

_____

_____

What lessons about fear did this experience teach you?

_____

_____

_____

_____

EVERYONE HAS FEAR

One of the main things to remember when fear arises within you is this: everyone has fears! The key is to accept this fact and move forward despite your fears. This, I believe, is the true meaning of courage.

If you feel confused and frightened before beginning something, think of Christopher Columbus in 1492. When he started, he didn't know where he was going. When he got there, he didn't know where he was. And when he returned to Spain, he didn't know where he had been. Plus he had made his great sailing voyages all on borrowed money.

Here's a more recent example. In my opinion, I don't think anyone in modern history put his fears aside and went out on a limb more than the late Dr. Martin Luther King, Jr. Dr. King concluded his last speech on April 3, 1968, in Memphis, Tennessee, with these words:

> "Well, I don't know what will happen now. We've got some difficult days ahead. But it doesn't really matter with me now, because I've been to the mountaintop and I don't mind. Like anybody, I would like to live a long life. Longevity has its place. But I'm not concerned about that now. I just want to do God's will, and He's allowed me to go up to the mountain. And I've looked over and I've seen the Promised Land. And I'm happy tonight; I'm not worried about anything. I'm not fearing any man. Mine eyes have seen the glory of the coming of the Lord!"[10]

We all know the tragic fate of Dr. King. What's important to remember is that he put his fear aside and did what his heart told him to do. And because of that, he is arguably one of the most important leaders to have ever lived because of his human rights accomplishments that reverberated around the globe.

Martin Luther King, Jr. was an amazing man of God. I am certain that because of his faith, he was better prepared to minimize his fears. Dr. King's work reminds me of Reverend Dick Gregory's words:

> "Fear and God do not occupy the same space."[11]

EXERCISE

Think for a moment, then list dreams or activities that you have thought about doing at some point but have never begun or completed because of fear or apprehension:

_____

_____

_____

_____

_____

_____

Once you have listed these, circle the ones that you still have time to accomplish when you overcome your fears.

PUTTING YOUR FEARS ASIDE

To succeed in life and reach your destiny, you must develop belief and trust in yourself. French novelist Anatole France said:

"To accomplish great things we must not only act,
but also dream; not only plan, but also believe."[12]

Only when you trust your abilities and believe in yourself can you overcome your fears and leap into whatever it is that your heart is calling you to do. Here's a quote from Mary Anne Radmacher that I feel represents this point well:

"The jump is so frightening between where I am and where I want to be . . . because of all I may become, I will close my eyes and leap!"[13]

I know, I know—trusting yourself is easier said than done. Just like Christopher Columbus and Martin Luther King, Jr., however, you must learn to put your fears aside and pursue what it is that you want to accomplish. Here are some specific ways I've found to reduce or eliminate fear. I call this my "fear destruction process."

FEAR DESTRUCTION PROCESS

- Understand that you only live on earth *one time*. Thus, you must make every moment count.

- Study the true risk of the situation at hand. How much fear is legitimate and how much is a matter of your own mind?

- Ask yourself, "If I don't do this, will it haunt me for the rest of my life?" Regret is one of the most disappointing and disheartening human emotions.

- Ask yourself, "Is there something that I fear that must be overcome if I am to reach my goals?" Often, focusing on what we can obtain, such as goals, helps us to reduce fear.

- Ask yourself, "Could the task at hand get me killed?" I know this sounds extreme, but it helps put things in perspective.

Now I'm going to share two examples in my life in which I had to overcome fear to really break through a barrier to accomplish my goals (one family-related, the other career-related).

My family travels to Maui every February and we stay at Kaanapali Beach. At the far north end of Kaanapali Beach, there's a huge rock and cliff formation that protrudes out into the ocean about a quarter of a mile. This area is also one of the best snorkeling spots in all of Maui, if not all of Hawaii. The cliff is called "Black Rock," and many of the local kids jump or dive off this 30-foot cliff for fun. Well, after watching this for several days, my son, Sam, who was nine at the time, decided that he and his father (that's me) were going to jump off this cliff into the ocean below. Later that day my wife overheard Sam telling some other kids at the pool what we were going to do. Well, to say the least, I hate jumping from high places, regardless of how deep the water is.

At this point, I realized that I'd never shared with my son the story of the time I climbed up the headwall of Mount Washington (one of the highest mountains east of the Mississippi). It was during the summer of 1981. I was 12 years old, and my sister and I went on a hiking vacation with some friends in the White Mountains of New Hampshire. At one point on this trip, my 13-year-old friend and I took a shortcut away from the others and soon found ourselves perched on the headwall of Mount Washington like two baby eagles in their nest. We were traversing the edge of a cliff on a trail about 12 inches wide and had to maneuver 100 feet to the other side to get to safety. This cliff, which had claimed many lives, dropped more than 1,000 feet straight down. I was scared to death since I could have easily fallen and lost my life. We safely made it to the other side, going very slowly without the use of ropes. At that point in my life, I decided that never again would I ever find myself positioned at the top of a cliff—regardless of the circumstances.

Being presented with both the challenge of jumping off this cliff in Maui and my son's questioning of my manliness, I found myself evaluating this potential jump from every angle. Here is what came to me:

- I realized that you only live once, and that I was, after all, on vacation.

- I studied the level of risk involved. I had seen many kids jump off that cliff, and no one had hit any rocks below. I even watched them enter the water from below the surface through my snorkel mask.

- I then asked myself, "If I don't do this, what will my son think of me?" Well, obviously he'd think that I was a wimp. But I wanted him to view me as a *hero* . . . just as I view my own dad, a golfer, who has made three holes-in-one in his lifetime!

- If I am to be adventurous, as one of my life goals indicates, then I should jump.

- Finally, I concluded that if I jumped out as far as I could, then I would certainly miss the side of the cliff and land in the water. I may hit the water awfully hard, but I knew I would *live*.

With this due diligence behind me, my son and I both jumped off Black Rock. In fact, we did it twice. Let me tell you, it was quite a rush. My wife took pictures of both of us in mid-air, and they turned out great. My son thinks I am a hero for jumping and we will share this incredible memory together forever. Now, I jump at least one time each and every year that we visit Maui.

The reason that I share this experience is to ask you: what cliffs do you face in your life that you must jump from, to get from where you are now, to where you want to go?

Speaking of heroes, my wife and I have another wonderful son named Jacob. When he was a young child, we used to take him to the beach frequently to look for crabs under the rocks. He soon learned that the bigger the rocks were, the more crabs there would be hidden underneath. As a result, we turned over small rocks, then bigger rocks, then we somehow turned over even bigger rocks. As we did this, he would get more and more excited because he would see more crabs each time as the rocks got bigger. He then pointed to a huge boulder (almost the size of a minivan) and said, "Dad, if you could pick up that rock, then you would be my hero." I was not able to lift up that boulder, but I will always remember this moment that we shared together.

The question that I would like to ask those of you who are parents is this: what can you do in your life to become your child's hero? Understand that in many cases, in order to become your child's hero, you may need to overcome your fears.

Here's my career-related example about overcoming fear: I spent four years going back and forth as to whether or not I should hunker down and finish this book. I finally realized that the true risk to my career was to not follow through with what my heart had told me to do. My heart had told me that this book and my speaking career were my passions, and that if I was to be truly happy and fulfilled in life, then I *must* make this happen. If I hadn't listened to this internal message, two things could have happened:

1. I could have spent the rest of my days regretting my lack of action (or inaction) and I'd always be disappointed in myself for not living up to my full potential.

2. I'd be stuck with only a sales career and making a decent living. In other words, I'd be building wealth for someone else instead of for my family. I would then question myself as to why I had limited my options to just "a job," when I could have accomplished so much more.

It is only natural to let fear get in your way and to question yourself and wonder what others will think of you as you pursue your goals. Les Brown said that you should:

> "Never let someone else's opinion of you
> become your reality."[14]

Don't worry about what other people think of you and your aspirations. No one but you can measure the size and strength of your heart.

If your heart is telling you what your passion is, then follow it and great things will happen in your life. I'm confident of this.

PAIN AND PLEASURE

Putting your fears aside can be a very painful experience. I'll be the first to admit this fact, because I've known my share of pain. But pain can be a positive. Before I explain how, here's a quick story:

A mailman delivered mail to an old man who sat on his porch with his dog. Every day the mailman wondered why the dog was moaning. Finally the mailman asked the old man this question, and the old man replied, "There's a nail sticking up from the porch that's jabbing him in the side." The mailman said, "Well then, why doesn't your dog get up and move?" to which the old man replied, "Well, I guess it doesn't hurt him enough to make him move."

Many pains are like the one that dog experienced—pains that are small and nagging but not strong enough to motivate us. Well-known speaker and motivational coach Anthony Robbins says that human motivations stem from two main sources: our desire to either avoid pain or gain pleasure.

If you have something jabbing you in the side of life, don't be afraid and sit there and moan like that old dog. I challenge you to get up and do something about your pain and take the necessary action or actions to control your circumstances. I guarantee that if you do, you will be one step closer to creating your own destiny.

SUMMARY

Overcoming your fears is difficult. I'm not going to say it isn't. Think, for example, of all I went through before I jumped off that cliff. Now think of the cliffs you face in life that are keeping you from achieving your goals. Then ask yourself again—what cliffs do you need to jump off to move forward in life and become the type of person you want to be?

With a much more severe consequence than cliff jumping, Martin Luther King, Jr. put his fears aside and did what was right despite what he knew could ultimately happen. He lost his life in the process, but ultimately freed millions of people from oppression.

Neil Armstrong and the other astronauts aboard Apollo 11 had no guarantees that they would safely return home to earth when they boarded the spacecraft aimed at the moon. Heroes such as Martin Luther King, Jr. and Neil Armstrong prove to us that, regardless of our fears, we can overcome them and achieve great things.

Eliminating or even greatly reducing fear must take place for you to continue to move forward in the pursuit of your goals and your destiny. Review my fear destruction process whenever you feel frozen with fear.

I can think of no better message of plowing forward in life in pursuit of your goals despite your level of fear, than what Frank Herbert said:

> "I must not fear.
> Fear is the mind-killer.
> Fear is the little-death that
> brings total obliteration.
> I will face my fear.
> I will permit it to pass over me
> and through me.
> And when it has gone past, I will
> turn the inner eye to see its path.
> Where the fear has gone
> there will be nothing.
> Only I will remain."[15]

What I believe he means is that when we face our fears, we learn to somehow overcome them. Then we are no longer fearful. In the process of going through these struggles, we become more confident in every area of life.

My belief is that your heart knows what is best for you, so you need to listen to this calling and move forward, pursuing whatever your heart is calling you to—despite your fears. It is okay to be afraid, just as long as you make certain that your fear does not stop you. I challenge you to listen to your heart, put your fears aside, and go.

Finally, I encourage you to turn your fears into fuel. I challenge you to jump from your cliff and grow wings on the way down. In doing so, you will be well on your way to overcoming your fears and creating your own destiny.

CHAPTER 8

Remembering Those Who Molded You

Who, being loved, is poor?
—Oscar Wilde[1]

Now that you have a positive and grateful understanding of the people and things that you're blessed with in life and know that the down times are only temporary, you're free to pursue your destiny—a destiny that will be very different from anyone else's. But please remember this important point: as you pursue your goals, don't forget who the truly important people are in your life—your family and your close friends.

We often get so caught up in pursuing our dreams and reaching our destiny that we sometimes forget these important people. While you pursue your goals, you must stop and remember that to be loved, you must love. After all, love is a verb.

The following poem, written by Charles Hanson Towne, left quite an impression on me:

Around the corner I have a friend

In this great city that has no end.

Yet the days go by and the weeks rush on,

And before I know it a year is gone!

And I never see my old friend's face,

For life is a swift and terrible race.

He knows I like him just as well,

As in the days when I rang his bell.

And he rang mine, though we were younger then,

And now we are busy tired men.

Tired of playing a foolish game,

Tired of trying to make a name.

"Tomorrow," I say, "I will call Jim,"

Just to show that I'm thinking of him.

But tomorrow comes and tomorrow goes,

And the distance between us grows and grows.

Around the corner—yet miles away,

Here's a telegram, sir: "Jim died today."

And that is what we get and deserve in the end,

Around the corner, a vanished friend!²

Remember to always say what you mean. If you love someone, tell them. Don't be afraid to express yourself. Reach out and tell that someone what they mean to you. Because when you decide that it is the right time, it may be too late! Seize the day; never have regrets. Most importantly, stay close to your friends and family, for they helped make you the person you are today!

This is a very touching poem—after all, your friends and family are the ones who can bring more *love* into your life, if you stay close to them over the years. Everyone yearns for more *love*, so always try to keep in touch with your loved ones.

FRIENDS MAKE A DIFFERENCE

My best friend is a guy named Dave Beauchamp. We've known each other since the third grade. In fact, my mother and

EXERCISE

Who are the people—family, friends, and acquaintances—that have made a difference in your life?

_____

_____

_____

_____

_____

What steps can you take to reach out to each of these people on a regular basis?

_____

_____

_____

_____

_____

Are there any people in your life who are in need in some way? If so, what can you do to help?

_____

_____

_____

_____

_____

his father went to high school together in the 1950s in Flint, Michigan. Back when my family's house burned, it was Dave and his mother, Kathy, who organized a school food drive for our family (Kathy was an extremely caring and loving person—like a second mother to me until she passed away in May 1985). We had just moved out of a hotel and into a rental home for the summer, and I can remember my mother's tears of joy as Dave and his mother delivered at least 30 bags of groceries to our temporary home while our house was being repaired.

After college, I helped Dave by forwarding his resume to someone I knew. That person later hired him.

Dave and I continue to be close today. In fact, a month never goes by without one of us calling the other. In 1996, Dave came to Seattle on a business trip. At the time, I was deliberating as to whether to return to public speaking and was even pondering writing a book. Dave encouraged me. "You have a good story to tell," he said, "and people will read it."

I have always cherished his words and have used them as an inspiration along my journey. Thank you, Dave. The friendships we nurture help us get more *happiness* in our lives. Our friendship reminds me of what Abraham Lincoln said in 1849:

"The better part of one's life consists of his friendships."[3]

Dave's words inspired me to write this book. If you, too, have a good story to tell and desire to become a published author, please visit my web site www.CreateYourOwnDestiny.com and click on "Publishing Help" to see how I can help you become published. Through Dave and my speaking coach, Albert Mensah, I learned that people want to be entertained in life through stories (movies, books, video games, etc.).

I encourage you to never forget all those great times and stories you have shared with your family and friends over the years. Ultimately, someday, all that we have left will be our stories. This is one reason I love speaking to older folks so much. I love to listen and learn from their stories and wisdom.

Like Dave and Albert have done for me, I would like you to think of others in your life in addition to your close friends who may have encouraged you as well; maybe a coach or a teacher or possibly a minister.

Two other men I would like to acknowledge for their efforts in molding me are Bill McCarrick and Rob Van Pelt. Bill coached me in football and baseball through elementary and junior high school. Rob coached me in football and basketball in high school. Both of these men worked for schools near my hometown, but they also coached as a way of giving something back to their community. These two taught me what competition and team work are all about. They also taught me that winning isn't everything, but what's most important is putting forth your best effort in an attempt to win. This is really the definition of success. Both men always inspired me to go the extra mile and not fall into the trap of mediocrity. Both have wonderful families of their own, yet they always treated me like one of their sons.

Because of the principles that these two wonderful men instilled in me at a young age, I was able to take this knowledge and confidence with me into the business world. When I had my back injury early in college (which ended my football career), I grew from that experience because of what these two coaches taught me. I was able to transfer my athletic discipline into my academics, and later, my career.

Because of this knowledge, I feel that I have a tremendous advantage over my competition in the business world. Thank you Bill. Thank you Rob. They are two great men. In fact, Rob Van Pelt taught me the difference between winning and losing with this statement:

> "The difference between winners and losers is that
> winners show up expecting to win, while losers
> show up hoping to win."

Because of them, today I help coach my kids' youth football team. I also spent many years coaching lacrosse, baseball, and basketball. I try to instill in these children the same messages that they once taught me. I can only hope that my children will get to play someday for someone like Bill and Rob.

EXERCISE

Think of a friend who has helped you with words and support. What can you do to say "thank you" to this friend?

_____

_____

_____

_____

Now think of other close friends: What can you do to help inspire and support them?

_____

_____

_____

_____

FAMILY MAKES A DIFFERENCE

All of us have that someone special in our lives, be it a mother or a grandparent. The question then must be, what are you doing (or what can you do) to show that person you are grateful for what they have done for you over the years to make you the person you are today? My parents have both recently retired and, like many retired couples in good health, they are somewhat concerned about their long-term financial situation. I can't even imagine how much money they spent on me from birth through college, but I have a deep desire to help them out in return in any way I can. They have told me that they do not need my help, but I still have a desire to do so in one way or another. However, you don't need to compensate or "repay" those who molded you. Instead, how about writing nice two-page letters from your heart thanking the people for all they have done for you. You'll be surprised how appreciative this message will be in their eyes.

Lastly, visit your family as often as possible or help them visit you. Accept them for who they are and, whatever you do, *don't* try to change them. Love them for who they are and always be grateful for what they have done for you.

I have also learned how powerful and comforting it can be to speak with my parents often over the phone and continually seek out their advice.

SUMMARY

Remembering those who helped mold you is an important part of being able to give something back in life. What's more, you can use your positive experiences from people who have helped you in your efforts to help others. The world will truly be a better place if we think of ourselves less, and instead think about—and assist—others as much as possible. Zig Ziglar said:

> "You can have everything in life that you want,
> if you will just help enough other people get what they want."[4]

Ziglar's quote is so true. People will only care how much you know when they know how much you care. Never forget those who helped mold you along the way. If you can't find a way to make it up to them, mentor a young person and show them the way, just as someone once did for you. This person will be eternally grateful for your time and energy. One of the best investments we can all make is to spend time with the youth of today, because they will become the leaders of tomorrow.

Remember, we are incapable of changing another human being regardless of how much we may want to. This reminds me of Mahatma Gandhi's famous quote:

"You must be the change you wish to see in the world."[5]

Finally, I encourage you to get a photo of each person who has positively impacted your life, frame these pictures, and place them on a wall in your home office. This will become your "wall of fame" and serve as a reminder of those who molded you.

SECTION THREE

EXECUTE

❧

I will do today,
what others don't,
so I will have tomorrow,
what others won't.
—John Addison[1]

CHAPTER 9

Executing Your Plan Daily

Energy and persistence conquer all things.
—Benjamin Franklin[2]

Up to this point we have done a lot of dreaming, planning, goal setting, and laying the financial and motivational groundwork for our destiny. But planning is never enough—at some point you must act.

Not all actions are physical actions. They can be mental as well. Mental actions are called *decisions* and are as important in creating your own destiny as are physical actions.

My father always told me that when faced with a situation or opportunity, not making a decision to act is actually a decision to not do anything at all.

You have heard (I'm sure) the old proverb (also attributed to John Addison):

"He who hesitates is lost."[3]

It's similar to being in a car, waiting to pull out into traffic. If you spot an opening, you either stay or go. If you drive out halfway into traffic and *then* decide to pull back, or if you hesitate, you're more likely to be hit by another car. The same is true in life.

This reminds me of how I obtained a very lucrative job (lucrative because of the stock options). At the time, I wasn't really looking for a job, as I was happily employed by Toppan

Electronics. But a recruiter had been calling me over several weeks trying to get me excited about a sales position with Merix. Well, one day about 10:30 AM, I received a call from John Cavanaugh, a sales manager at Merix. He was in town and his lunch appointment had just been cancelled, so he called to ask if I would be interested in meeting with him for lunch as an informal first interview. At first I declined, thinking, "Why should I spend an hour in the car (each way) to meet someone from another organization when I am very content with my current position?" I hung up the phone, then thought: *he who hesitates in life, loses!* I immediately called him back to confirm our lunch appointment.

To make a long story short, that first lunch appointment laid the foundation for me eventually getting a job offer. This was the first job where I made over six figures in annual salary and commissions, and it was the first one to give me a significant amount of stock options as well (all because I didn't hesitate). Instead, I took immediate action. I had only been off the phone for about two seconds before calling him back. I went after the opportunity that had been presented to me. Your opportunity may also appear this quickly, so it is important not to hesitate, instead execute immediately.

Opportunities are never lost. They are just found by other people who take quick action.

You can also think of taking action another way. I'm sure you've copied songs from various artists onto a tape or CD. The songs are all there, ready to be heard. But it's only when you press the "play" button that you can hear the music, the fruit of your efforts. That's what taking action is: hitting the "play" button in your life.

I know what many of you are probably thinking right now: "I'm too busy," or, "That's easy for you to say, but I have two jobs, a spouse, kids, and other responsibilities that take up my time." Or, "I take evening classes, so I don't have the time."

All of us have time constraints. The key is to accept this and still move forward, even if you do only a little bit each day. Here's an old saying that might help you: *yard by yard, life is hard; inch by inch, life's a cinch!* Henry Ford said:

> "Nothing is particularly hard if you
> divide it into small jobs."[4]

It doesn't matter how fast you are moving toward your goals. The key is that you are moving toward your goals steadily, on a daily basis, because, over time, this daily involvement will add up and produce results. Each daily action, no matter how small, will bring you one step closer to your destiny.

Still think you can't do something every day? Here are a few of the many things you can do each day to move closer to your destiny:

- Review your goals.

- Make a phone call or send an e-mail.

- Read a section from a motivational book or a book related to your destiny.

- Schedule one 15-minute session alone to brainstorm new ideas.

- Write for 20 minutes about something related to your destiny such as updating your resume, working on a business plan, or simply writing a letter to a potential client or partner.

- Edit and review something you have previously written.

- Research needed information on the Internet or at the library.

- Discuss your ideas with other like-minded people and build a team.

There are many, many ways to take action every day. This is critical to success, because action equals results. One of my favorite quotes regarding action comes from an unknown source:

"If you knew what you did today could change the way
you feel tomorrow, would you act differently?"

I guarantee that if you take some small actions every day toward your destiny, these small acts, when added up over five or ten years, will produce valuable results. In fact, I believe you'll not only meet your goals—you'll far exceed them.

Think about it this way—there is no such thing as overnight success. In fact, Susan Friedmann (an author friend of mine) shared this old adage with me:

"Overnight success takes ten to fifteen years!"

I believe that this is true if you do *one* action item per day in pursuit of your passion and destiny. Imagine, however, if you broke a sweat and you did *two* things per day in pursuit of your goals. You could achieve success in five to seven years. If you did *three* action items per day, it could happen in only three to five years.

For example, this book that you are reading is the result of nothing more than me writing a little bit here, a little bit there, in the early morning or late into the evening—over a five-year time frame. I began in 1996 and finished this in 2001. Since then, I have updated this book every year by adding new chapters. The original page count was 140, now it is 272. There were many times that several months would pass in which I didn't write at all because I got caught up in doing too many other things (including a vigorous travel schedule with my day job). But as you can see, the results of executing little by little over time can result in something significant. This book is now an international best seller and has helped thousands of people all over the world pursue their passions and create their own destinies. It happened for me and I am confident that your daily actions of executing your game plan will produce equally great results for you.

EXERCISE

Think of your goals and destiny, then list three ways you can execute your plan on any given day:

1. _____

2. _____

3. _____

TAKING RISKS

One potential drawback to taking action is the necessity, in many cases, of taking one or more risks. Taking a risk can be scary—there is the possibility of failing, of looking inept or unprepared.

But you must take risks in order to move toward your destiny. Here's another one of my favorite quotes, by T. S. Eliot, regarding risk taking:

> "Only those who will risk going too far
> can possibly find out how far one can go."[5]

I believe that if you are going to get what you want, then you must execute your plan and you can't wait for your ship to come in. I believe that when your ship does come in, it will not come all the way in to the shore. Think of all the cruise ships you see—many always stay anchored about one mile off shore when visiting small islands. When your ship comes in, you are going to have to muster the courage to leave the shore and swim out to it, if you want to reach your destiny.

A quote by Andre Gide further drives this point home:

> "Man cannot discover new oceans unless he
> has the courage to lose sight of the shore."[6]

EXERCISE

Reflect for a moment about a risk you faced at one time in your life. What fears or other emotions were present as you studied this risk?

_____

_____

_____

_____

_____

What either prevented you from moving forward or propelled you to act despite the risk?

_____

_____

_____

_____

_____

What lessons from this event can still help you when facing future risks?

_____

_____

_____

_____

_____

You must overcome risks to secure your destiny. Because this is the case, the true risk lies in not taking risks. Take educated risks. Don't worry about failing—that's just a word. There is no real failure in life—but there are lessons. Move forward embracing risks. You'll be happy with the results. You need to execute daily—despite risk.

I have literally risked every asset I had, and every asset I didn't have, to grow my business. In fact, due to my strong belief in my passions, I even risked our first home for the sake of my business—and it was the best risk I have ever taken. I have no regrets and would do it again to achieve these extraordinary results.

Nothing worthwhile in life comes without risk. Ask yourself this question: what are you willing to risk to get what you want?

FINDING MORE TIME

We've just discussed risk taking. Now I'd like to show you how to find more *time* in your day.

Whenever I discuss executing a plan on a daily basis, people almost always say the same thing: "Patrick, I don't have the time." Some people view this as a legitimate reason. I don't—I think this is an *excuse*.

If you truly don't have extra time in your life right now, then you *really* need to execute your plan and pursue a destiny that will give you more time later. If you fall into this category—where you use excuses not to do something—here are some ways to find more *time* on a daily basis to execute your game plan.

- Turn off the television. If you do watch TV, only watch programs related to your goals. For example, watch the Biography channel to learn how people you admire overcame tremendous odds and overwhelming adversities to achieve great things in their lives.

- Carry whatever book you are reading with you at all times. Then, when you find yourself with unexpected free time, such as waiting for someone to show up for an appointment, you won't waste that time—you can use it to read about your destiny-related topic.

- Carry a cell phone with you at all times. Again, this gives you the ability to make and receive calls during down or transition times, or at other moments where you normally might have wasted time.

- Limit small talk. It's fun to chat with friends and family. But too much small talk can steal precious moments from your day. Don't be impolite, but limit small talk as much as possible, especially at work—a good way to do this is to close your office door.

- Don't sleep in on weekends. A great time I've found to work on my dreams is on Saturday and Sunday mornings between 6 AM and 9 AM, before my kids are up and ready to go. The satisfaction of starting your day working toward your dreams is hard to describe.

- Limit Internet surfing. Don't surf unless you're looking for something specific to your goals or destiny. Your time is valuable; don't waste it online.

- Keep your computer free of viruses, annoying pop-up ads, and Internet hijackers. You can lose all kinds of time and productivity if you must continuously deal with these problems.

- Give up sports news. Sports scores and statistics can be addicting. Which would you rather be: someone who knows all the batting averages of the top 20 players in Major League Baseball, with no money in the bank, or a millionaire who doesn't know which team is most likely to win the Stanley Cup?

- Take control of your lunch hour. This can be an excellent time to work on your dream. Try to schedule a lunch meeting as often as possible with people you know are capable of helping you accomplish your dreams.

- Hire a housekeeper. This is an expense, of course. But the question to consider is this: where is your time more valuably spent—cleaning your bathroom or working on your dream?

- Quit playing video games. These games are addictive and if you aren't careful, video games can steal hours and hours of productivity from your weekly schedule. Also, some experts believe that smaller handheld games hurt or diminish your vision over time.

All these ideas will surely help you find more time in your day and week. Use this found time to execute your game plan. As stated earlier, it's important to realize that if you don't have any time *now*, you had better make certain that the successful implementation of your plan will give you more time *later*. Otherwise, twenty years will pass and you will be in the same situation that you are in now.

This reminds me of the rat race metaphor: if you ever watch a gerbil on a running wheel, you know what I'm talking about. A gerbil can get on that wheel and run like mad for 20 seconds (or even 20 minutes), only to get off and realize that it's in the exact same spot as when it began. Well, what is the difference between you and a gerbil? You could run on the corporate wheel (rat race) for 20 years and make little, if any, real "progress"—for instance, be in basically the same spot as when you started, although now you'll be 20 years older. Or, would you rather make time to pursue a destiny that will give you more *time*, more *money*, and more *freedom*?

To better understand the rat race concept, I recommend that you read two books by Robert Kiyosaki: *Rich Dad, Poor Dad* and *The Cashflow Quadrant*. Then play his game *Cashflow 101*, which teaches you that the only way to win in life is to get out of the rat race sooner rather than later.

EXECUTE TODAY AND BENEFIT TOMORROW

There's an old saying:

"If you do what you have always done, then you will get what you have always gotten."

If you are to truly become free, then you must execute your plan daily. Otherwise, you will one day die unfulfilled. That's not what I want for you—I want you to achieve all of your goals and your destiny.

Another thought: here's a humorous—but true—definition of insanity by Albert Einstein:

> "Insanity is doing the same thing over and over,
> and expecting different results."[7]

If you are to truly experience your destiny, then you must—without question—put your excuses and pains aside and execute your plan daily. As Bill McCarrick, the best football coach I ever had, used to say:

> "You have to play when you're hurt,
> if you want to win."[8]

Sooner or later, you will learn that all of those who have achieved tremendous feats in life have, at one time or another, "played hurt."

Pursuing your destiny and executing your plan daily is bound to "hurt" at times, but the rewards in terms of goals achieved and destinies created will be more than worth it!

DAILY EXECUTION

An example of my daily execution that I am sure I will never forget occurred in November 1994 when I had the opportunity to meet the President of the United States—Bill Clinton. Believe it or not, I was the one who made this happen. I knew that if I could put myself in the right spot, at the right time, a brief encounter would be inevitable. In other words, I turned an opportunity into a reality.

This is what happened: my family and I attended a very large church when we lived in Seattle. In the weeks before the encounter,

I learned that the President would be visiting the church during his trip campaigning for other Democrats prior to the 1994 elections. I marked my calendar book to make certain that I didn't miss service that weekend.

When I awoke that morning, I told my wife that I was going to meet the President that day. I made it a point to arrive 30 minutes early to ensure getting a center aisle seat, as I figured that he might walk down the center aisle at the conclusion of the service.

To make a long story short, the President made a side entrance, surrounded by at least a half dozen Secret Service agents. At the conclusion of the service, the President and his bodyguards exited the church via the center aisle where I was seated. He was moving at a speed that was almost a jog. It was obvious he was not stopping to shake anyone's hand, nor did he have any intention of doing so. But he had obviously not met Patrick Snow before.

Being the opportunist that I am, I wasn't content letting him walk by without a handshake. I stepped out into the aisle, leading with my right arm open—ready for a handshake. As I did this, all the Secret Service agents went for their guns. Once they determined that I was harmless, they backed off. I extended my arm to shake hands with the President and said, "My name is Patrick Snow, it is nice to meet you." He embraced my right hand with a firm handshake and then placed his left hand on my right forearm, and said "It's nice to meet you, Patrick."

As this occurred (unbeknownst to me), the church photographer took a picture of our handshake as we looked each other in the eye. The President then quickly rushed out the back of the church and jumped in his limousine (not shaking another hand along the way). To my surprise, this photo was placed on the front page of the church newspaper. I was given the original photo as a keepsake (it also helps prove to my friends that this brief encounter really occurred).

The point of this story is that because of my advance planning, preparation, and execution of my plan, I was able to make this dream unfold and become a reality. I simply saw the invisible (the future as I desired it to be) and consequently (because my actions were now almost second nature to me), I was able to achieve the impossible. Whether you know it or not, you, too, have this same ability. All you have to do to put this into action is believe in yourself and execute daily.

How many people can say that not only were they photographed with a President of the United States, but they also had their photo with the President on the front page of a newspaper? Can you imagine if I had decided to sleep in on that Sunday morning instead of meeting the President?

What could you accomplish if you woke up early every weekend? I have written (and rewritten) this book almost entirely during the morning hours on weekdays and weekends before my wife and children are awake.

I challenge you to execute each day as if you only had 30 days to live. You will be amazed at how much you can accomplish in such a short amount of time if you incorporate this sense of urgency. You will ultimately create your own destiny faster than you could have ever imagined.

SUMMARY

Daily execution of your game plan on a consistent basis is the most important key to successfully creating your own destiny in life. You must ask yourself: if you are not executing your plan daily, what goals you are not hitting, and what opportunities you are missing because of a lack of daily execution. Then ask yourself what is holding you back. Once you learn what your obstacles are, then do everything in your power to overcome them. If you find that a lack of knowledge or experience is holding you back, then either learn how to do the task at hand or hire someone more talented than you to get the job done right.

If you execute your plan daily over the course of five to ten years, I guarantee that you will not only meet all of your goals, you will far surpass them. This kind of achievement is what I call under-promising and over-delivering.

I will conclude this chapter with one of my favorite quotes from Mark Twain. It shows the importance of taking risks as you execute your plans in pursuit of your destiny:

"Twenty years from now you will be more disappointed by the things that you didn't do than by the ones you did do. So throw off the bowlines. Sail away from the safe harbor. Catch the trade winds in your sails. Explore. Dream. Discover."[9]

CHAPTER 10

Growing Your Business on a Limited Budget

Act boldly, and unseen forces will come to your aid.
—Brian Tracy[1]

Now what? Well, hopefully as a result of reading this book, you have come to the same conclusion I have: that it's virtually impossible to create your own destiny as an employee at a job. However, as a business owner, your chances of getting more *time*, more *money*, more *freedom*, more *health*, more *love*, and more *happiness* in life increase dramatically.

As I pointed out in Chapter 4, my solution for attaining wealth today is to own and operate your own business. Owning a business is not just a good idea; it is a necessity if you desire to get ahead and create long-term financial peace of mind as you plan for retirement. I sincerely believe what business consultant Brent Brodine says about this topic:

"Retiring with a million dollars is not a luxury, but a necessity."[2]

If you are reading this book and are a thriving business owner, feel free to skip this chapter and move on to the next. If you are already a small business owner but are *not* achieving the success you desire, then I'm confident you will receive great ideas and insights within this chapter.

If, however, you are unhappy at work and are looking to start your own business, or at least want to explore business ownership, then this chapter might be the most important chapter for you. If you have made it this far into the book and still don't know what kind of business to launch, I recommend that you visit my Web site, www.CreateYourOwnDestiny.com and click on "Free Stuff," then click on "50 Home-Based Business Ideas" to further help you sort through the many business opportunities you can pursue.

I hope you took the previous chapter to heart when I wrote that success may take longer than overnight. Well, launching a successful business is no different! I do believe, however, that anyone can be successful in launching a business if it is one they are passionate about and believe in. Successful businesses take time, money, energy, and, most of all, *action*—and *action* springs from passion.

In this chapter, I will show you how to take steps toward owning your own business without spending a bunch of money. Use this chapter as a blueprint to give you the best chance of being successful in your new business. I also recommend that you leverage the Internet and use it as a strategic resource to increase your business' chance of success. This chapter offers many strategies on how to successfully launch a new business, using the Internet as your business partner.

SEVEN DESIRABLE TRAITS FOR BUSINESS OWNERSHIP

In the course of appearing as a featured guest on hundreds of radio stations across North America (addressing unhappy workers), I am constantly asked what types of businesses are the best to pursue. I believe there is no one "right" business, but I do believe the best kinds of businesses share these seven desirable attributes. You are able to:

- Run them from the comfort of your home (on your schedule).

- Match them to your passions (you can't be successful doing something you don't enjoy).

- Operate them without having to hire employees (you don't want to be a babysitter).

- Get started with a low investment (franchises can cost hundreds of thousands of dollars).

- Make money whether you are working or sleeping (a Web store provides flexibility).

- Build the business without having to purchase huge amounts of inventory (garages are for cars).

- Utilize the Internet as your storefront to sell your products and services 24 hours per day, seven days a week, on a global basis.

I believe there are a million ways to make a million dollars. All it takes is for you to properly execute one way. While there are thousands of great businesses out there, many of which share the attributes just mentioned, to me three areas stand out: real estate investing (because of real estate appreciation), network marketing (due to teamwork and residual income), and perhaps my favorite, operating an Internet marketing business (with the resulting ability to reach the global marketplace 24/7).

ROAD MAP TO START A SUCCESSFUL BUSINESS

In Doug Hall's book, *Jump Start Your Business Brain*, Doug mentions that too many people get involved in business without first doing their due diligence. This due diligence gives them the best chances for success. In fact, Doug says that many people get involved in businesses when the odds are stacked against them. He says that you have a better chance of winning in a casino than succeeding in some business models. If you are going to gamble, he says that roulette offers your best bet, with odds at 47 percent.

I believe that if you follow these 20 suggestions (which I have developed over the years as a result of both my business successes and setbacks), your chances of success are far better than 47 percent.

If you skip over these, you might as well just go to a casino, where you may have better odds.

1. Pursue your most marketable passions.

2. Get emotional support from spouse (or family).

3. Perform a feasibility study.

4. Know your target market.

5. Take advantage of all tax deductions.

6. Minimize business expenses.

7. Focus on marketing.

8. Don't waste money on advertising.

9. Budget three times the money and time.

10. You may have to risk more than you think.

11. Align yourself with people more talented than you.

12. Grow your business through relationships and referrals.

13. Create a publicity buzz.

14. Determine your exit strategy.

15. Get a coach or mentor.

16. Join or create a mastermind group.

17. Determine your solution.

18. Leverage the Internet.

19. Get started.

20. Never give up until you win.

1. *Pursue your most marketable passions.* I believe it's virtually impossible to become successful building something in which you lack belief. If you are passionate about something, chances are

you'll stick with it through good times and bad. The best way to do this is to turn your hobbies into your business. Inventory your hobbies and ask yourself which could make money if you position your hobby as a business. Next, take the necessary steps to transition your hobby into your business.

2. *Get emotional support from spouse (or family)*. It is vitally important to receive support from your spouse or significant other early on in your business, because you will have to work long hours and, at the beginning, you may also have to spend more money than you make. With your spouse's blessing, you can work together toward achieving your vision. However, getting that blessing may be harder than you think, as there are a lot of cynics out there who do not believe it is possible to succeed in business. I recommend that you show your spouse examples of other people who have succeeded in business. In doing this, your spouse may come to realize that eventually he or she may be able to work out of choice, as opposed to working out of need—thanks to your business' success.

3. *Perform a feasibility study*. This is what you do prior to launching your business to ensure your success before getting started. It includes writing a business plan and creating a marketing plan (which are two different things). In your feasibility study, you will uncover the true costs of launching your business. Knowing this information from the beginning will increase your chances of success. This is one of the most important steps and should not be skipped.

4. *Know your target market*. It is extremely important to properly identify who exactly is going to purchase your product or service so that you can uncover their needs and use your solution to improve their life in one way or another. If you miss this step, you are almost certainly setting yourself up for failure. The best way to conduct market research is to interview potential buyers— ask people what they want and find out if they can get it. If they can't, perhaps your product or service can ease their pain.

5. *Take advantage of all tax deductions*. The free enterprise system in the United States is ideally suited for business owners,

but many overlook the many available tax deductions due to a lack of knowledge. For example, the following expenses are partially deductible for home-based business owners: mortgage payments, business expenses, computer expenses, mileage or vehicle usage, phone, utilities, Internet, and travel expenses.

6. *Minimize business expenses.* Growing a business can be very costly. But building this business (which becomes your asset) can support you for dozens of years to come. It can become one of the best investments that you ever make. Make capital expenditure decisions that will provide a solid return on your investment. Not all expenditures result in income. For many businesses, for example, advertising can be an unjustified expense.

7. *Focus on marketing.* Marketing is very effective and many times doesn't cost a lot of money. Marketing your business can take many different shapes and forms. The key is to maximize your efforts and expand your reach to as many people as possible. For example, it does not cost money to post flyers or put business cards on community bulletin boards. One of the best marketing experts in the world is Dan Kennedy. I encourage you to visit his web site, www.DanKennedy.com, and read his books to become a marketing expert.

8. *Don't waste money on advertising.* Advertising can cost a lot of money and many times is ineffective. When my destiny message was featured as the cover story of *USA TODAY* on December 5, 2002, I learned that marketing flat out works. However, in that same issue, I am sure there were business owners who had spent thousands of dollars placing ads in the back of the paper and may not have received any calls. Stay clear of advertising salespeople unless you have an unlimited budget. The following is a perfect example to help you distinguish the difference between marketing and advertising. Suppose that you list your web site with search engines—spending money doing so would be good *marketing* dollars spent. However, listing your web address on another web site as an *advertisement* would be advertising dollars spent and would, in my opinion, be a waste of money.

9. *Budget three times the money and time.* If you think that you are going to be able to invest $5,000 in your business and make tons of money in the first six months, you may be correct. If you plan on this allocation, keep in mind that your investment may ultimately end up being $15,000, and it may take 18 months to receive huge returns. The reason that this is important is, ultimately, your business may take longer than you want for it to become successful, costing you more money as a result. However, I can assure you that this extra time and money is a good investment and will help you attain the kind of freedom a business can provide.

10. *You may have to risk more than you think.* Nothing worthwhile in life comes without risk. Howard Schultz risked every asset he had, and even assets he didn't have, to launch Starbucks. Today Starbucks is a multi-billion dollar company; and, Schultz was able to purchase the Seattle Supersonics, which he later sold. The bottom line is this: successful people take risks. If you want to become wealthy, then you, too, must take risks. Ask yourself this question: what are you willing to risk to get what you want?

11. *Align yourself with people more talented than you.* The smartest business owners hire people even more intelligent than themselves to help grow their business. Once your team is in place, then you must delegate. Additionally, if you don't know how to do something, then contract that work out, such as your tax preparation. A great place to meet extremely talented people is to attend or join local networking groups. You will find that networking groups are filled with successful entrepreneurs. You may not hire them as full-time employees, but you can certainly seek their assistance to help you grow your business.

12. *Grow your business through relationships and referrals.* You must develop relationships with prospects to close sales. To do so, you must gain the trust and respect of those prospects, as well as qualify their needs; as I outlined in my sales success formula in Chapter 4. Zig Ziglar says: "If people like you, they'll listen to you, but if they trust you, they'll do business with you."[3] Bottom line is this: people buy from whom they like. When you make more

friends, you make more sales. It's that simple. Encourage satisfied customers to help you attract more business. Reward your clients when they give you qualified leads. Doing this, you can eventually create a complete business by referral. Brian Buffini's referral program teaches small business owners to host "client appreciation dinners" as a way of keeping leads coming in. Buffini's site is www. ProvidenceSeminars.com.

13. *Create a publicity buzz.* In Truett Cathy's book, *Eat Mor Chikin: Inspire More People*, the founder discusses how his company, Chick-fil-A, spent a small amount of money on clever billboards around Atlanta displaying images of cows painting the billboard, which read: "Eat Mor Chikin," and, "Five Out of Five Cows Agree." As a result, his company received millions of dollars worth of free publicity via radio, newspapers, and TV because Chick-fil-A had successfully created a publicity buzz. This is the kind of thing that gets media attention. Do something creative like this, then pitch your press releases to the media.

14. *Determine your exit strategy.* The goal is retirement, plain and simple. When do you want to retire, and with how much money? Many people never put a time frame on this objective. I believe it is important to understand how much money you will need to be able to retire. More importantly, set a date for your retirement and walk away. Ideally, you will want your business to create a residual income that will allow you to continue to make money long after retirement.

15. *Get a coach or mentor.* It is easier and more economical to learn from other people's mistakes than to repeat them yourself. For this reason, I believe it is crucial to find people you can trust who are in business for themselves and ask them to help you as you launch your business. You will be surprised by how many people are willing to help if you only ask. Business coaches come in all flavors. I encourage you to also visit a networking group in your area where you'll find local coaches willing to help you out. A national coaching organization worth looking into is called Building Champions. Their web site is www.BuildingChampions.com.

16. *Join or create a mastermind group*. Napoleon Hill is the father of the mastermind concept. In his book, *Law of Success*, he states that a mastermind group can be created by bringing two or more minds together in the spirit of harmony. This "blending of the minds" creates a "third mind," which may be appropriated and used by one or all of the individual minds. This process, or "third mind," will provide insights or ideas that may not come to light without such a mastermind group. I am in two mastermind groups and both have been very beneficial to my growth as an entrepreneur.

17. *Determine your solution*. It is important to know the value proposition of your product or service. In other words, what problem does your product or service solve for your clients? This is important to identify in order for your business to be successful. If you don't know what need your product or service meets in the market, then you may never succeed in business. Your company must solve other people's needs. In doing so, your clients will tell others about you, and your company will continue to grow.

18. *Leverage the Internet*. You can't be everywhere all the time. For that reason, it is important to leverage the Internet by having a solid web site with a high ranking on a search engine to bring prospects to your web store. More details on web sites, the Internet, and search engines follow later in this chapter. However, if you are not a technical person, I highly encourage you to leverage another person or company's expertise and have them build and maintain your site instead of spending time doing this yourself. You could spend thousands of hours building and maintaining your site, but this is time you could be marketing your business instead. I encourage you to evaluate the next section on the huge increases in the number of web sites worldwide (which royal.pingdom.com currently estimates at more than 162 million and growing rapidly).

19. *Get started*. Getting started in business can be a scary proposition, so much so that we must develop a high level of courage to overcome our fears and move forward. This concept reminds me of one of my favorite quotes from an unknown source: "courage is the ability to let go of the familiar." Get a business

license, set up your company's legal structure, and start saving all your receipts for taxes. Once this is done, make sure that you accomplish something each day for your business. Too many people get started in business and then take a few weeks off here and there and then never get back on track.

20. *Never give up until you win.* Too many people give up on their dreams just inches shy of their gold mine. The world is filled with people who gave up too soon and who now remain dependent on their jobs to support their families. Business ownership is one of the best ways to attain wealth. However, to accomplish your goals, you must stay the course the entire way and remain committed.

The Internet

The Internet continues to experience explosive growth by people of all ages and levels of business experience, from the novice to the computer savvy. There is a reason why there are currently more than 162 million web sites worldwide: millions of people from all corners of the earth have found a better way to sell products and services than through traditional storefronts, which can be very costly.

A Special Note

It used to be common knowledge that to be successful in business it took three things: location, location, and location. Today, this may still be true for a traditional business, but perhaps now more important than location is: presence on the Internet. With a good web site and online merchant store, your company can be accessible by every person worldwide with Internet access. This kind of coverage transcends location.

However, to get a good location for your web site, you will need to use search engines to ensure high placement of your site. This can be challenging if you don't know what you are doing. I encourage you to have your webmaster help you out with search engine placement. Many webmasters are good at *building* sites, but not at *placing* sites. If this is the case in your situation, I have identified a resource to help you with search engine placement and optimization: Stores Online (www.StoresOnline.com) helps small businesses secure high web placements on search engines.

In the interviews that you will read at the end of this chapter, you will find that virtually all of the business owners recommend securing a high placement on a search engine in order to grow a successful Internet business.

EXERCISE

In the space below, list five products or services that you are passionate about and can market using the Internet:

1. _____

2. _____

3. _____

4. _____

5. _____

UNIQUE SELLING PROPOSITION

When deciding what kinds of products or services to sell on the Internet, it is important to ask yourself why people will buy your product or service instead of your competitor's. You need to determine what Doug Hall calls a "unique selling proposition" so that you can set yourself apart from the others.[4]

For example, if you decide to sell calculators on the Internet, you had better come up with a darn good reason why people should buy *your* calculators when they could just as easily go to a local office supply store and pick one up the same day.

As a professional speaker and author, I try to set myself apart from the other speakers by informing meeting planners when they pay my full speaking fee. I cover all of my transportation costs and meals. Most speakers try to nickel-and-dime a meeting planner to death, trying to get upgrades on flights, limo rides to and from the airport, as well as dining in expensive restaurants on their dime. I cover all these expenses, and because of this, meeting planners have a more enjoyable experience booking me to speak instead of my competition.

EXERCISE

Think of one of your favorite companies and list three reasons why you buy from them instead of buying from their competition:

1. _____

2. _____

3. _____

Now write down three reasons why people will buy your product or service (these reasons become your Unique Selling Proposition):

1. _____

2. _____

3. _____

SUCCESSFUL INTERNET AND WEB SITE STRATEGIES

If you were to get into a traditional business, you would be very concerned as to the appearance, location, signage, and cleanliness of your establishment. Well, an Internet marketing business is no different—your web site serves as your storefront.

Over the years, I have learned to implement many of the strategies I'm about to share. As a result, my site, www.Create YourOwnDestiny.com, currently gets more hits than I could have ever imagined a few years ago. If you implement the following strategies for your web site, you will increase your chances of success.

1. Decide your first and second most desired response.

2. Secure a domain name that is easy to remember.

3. Get your site listed with many search engines.

4. Provide something for free.

5. Simplify your site.

6. Have 10 to 12 items on your navigation bar.

7. Provide a newsletter sign-up.

8. Never sell e-mail addresses to anyone.

9. Send out newsletters on a regular basis.

10. Always provide "Home" option.

11. Use third-party endorsements on your home page.

12. Place your photo and video on your site.

13. Have e-commerce set up to accept credit cards.

14. List your web address on everything.

15. Have a counting device on your site.

16. Evaluate which pages are being visited the most.

17. Ask visitors for feedback.

18. Provide "Zoom-In" capability.

19. Use a consistent color scheme.

20. Do not rely solely on search engines for traffic.

1. *Decide your first and second most desired responses.* The goal of your web site must be clearly communicated to your webmaster (or whoever is building your site). I have visited plenty of great sites that educate me but don't drive me to their web store to buy. When people want to buy from you, your site must make it easy to do so. For example, your first desired response may be to sell your products or services, so make that the goal of your site. Your second desired response may be to collect names and e-mail addresses so that you can build a database. Whatever your goals are for your site, *it is absolutely crucial that you communicate these goals to your webmaster.* It is better to have a functional web site that accomplishes your objectives than a really cool web site with flash animation that doesn't sell your products or services.

2. *Secure a domain name that is easy to remember.* "Domain name" is just another name for "web site." An easy-to-remember domain name is always best. It should be something that is memorable, and ends with "dot com." You don't want your prospects to have a difficult time remembering your site address. Fewer words are better than more. Additionally, you may have five or six different domain names pointing to the same web site. Also, make sure that you get your first and last name "dot com." If someone else has your name and has a site, contact them and perhaps they will sell it to you. The reason why you want an easy name to remember is so that when you start marketing your site, prospects can see your flyer and remember your web site address without having to write it down. A bad domain name would be either lengthy or difficult to remember and may be "dot biz," "dot net," and so forth. The most recognizable domain ending is "dot com." Also, you want to stay away from slashes in your address as it is just too hard to remember.

3. *Get your site listed with many search engines.* Search engines are systems on the Internet that list web sites in a specific order for visitors to view sites. Yahoo!, Google, MSN, and Lycos are popular search engines. It is important to get your site listed on these engines if you are trying to sell products and services on the Internet. This can cost a bit of money to set up, so if you don't know what you are doing, you are better off hiring someone to help you complete this task. A web expert can create "spider words" and embed them into your home page. Then, when visitors place these words in a search engine, your web site will be listed. Not only is it important to be listed, you really want a high listing since most people surfing the Web only go about ten sites deep when searching.

4. *Provide something for free.* Everyone wants something for free. Many people who surf on the Web are just entertaining themselves and have no desire to buy anything. You want these folks to refer your site to others. The best way that I have found to do this is to offer many freebies on my site. I give away at least a dozen free reports and different kinds of goal sheets. As a result, I frequently get e-mails from others telling me how much they appreciated my free stuff and they have told others about my site. Ideally, the free stuff that you give away should be something that people can download. You don't want to even think about getting in the business of shipping free stuff.

5. *Simplify your site.* The problem with many sites today is that visitors can get overwhelmed with information. In fact, they can spend so much time navigating a web site they never get to the web store to purchase anything. Simple is always better than complex. Also, a simple web site doesn't cost nearly as much as complex sites cost to build. In other words "dumb it down." Make sure that someone with a sixth-grade reading level can adequately navigate your site.

6. *Have 10 to 12 items on your navigation bar.* A navigation bar is another way of identifying your web site's table of contents. This ties closely to the previous point: you don't want 20 things that your

visitors can look at on your site, because they may leave without having gotten to your web store. I believe 10 to 12 items on your main page is ideal. I have the following items on my site: Home, Free Stuff, Publishing Help, Highlight Video, Client List, Book Reviews, Webucation, Fee Schedule, Speaking Calendar, Biz Opportunity, JV Affiliates, Web Store, Press Room, Contact Patrick, and a newsletter sign-up option.

7. *Provide a newsletter sign-up.* On every page of your site you should provide an option for visitors to sign up for your news-letter. Then, to take this a step further, you should not allow your visitors to gain access to your Free Stuff until they have inserted their e-mail address in the section that signs them up for your newsletter. I have done this for years and have grown my database from almost nothing to several thousand using this technique. You may wonder how many people unsubscribe from my newsletter. My experience is that every time I send out a newsletter, less than one-tenth of 1 percent unsubscribe. Creating a database of your prospects and customers is one of your most important goals as a business owner.

8. *Never sell e-mail addresses to anyone.* Not only should you mention this as a disclaimer on your site, but also make sure that you never sell or give your e-mail databases to anyone. You want to establish credibility and build trust with your clients by keeping their e-mail addresses confidential. Without having this disclaimer in small print, many visitors may want to sign up, but may be reluctant due to their concerns about getting spam from other sources.

9. *Send out newsletters on a regular basis.* Newsletters are a very good way to communicate with your prospects and customers. However, make sure your newsletter has something of value to your readers. You can't send out the same newsletter each time just reminding them to buy from you. If you provide newsworthy or interesting information, then you can always pitch your message at the bottom of your newsletter. For example, I always provide five thought-provoking quotes at the very beginning of my newsletter.

In doing so, I have had many respond to tell me how much they enjoyed the quotes. Additionally, it is important to include an easy-to-find "Unsubscribe" option in each newsletter so that if people no longer want your newsletter, they can easily remove their names. Finally, you want to make sure that your company stays in front of your prospects, but don't hammer them too often with a newsletter. Some believe that daily or weekly newsletters are good. However, I believe that every-other-week or monthly may be better so as not to annoy your subscribers.

10. *Always provide a "Home" option.* The "Home" option takes visitors to your home page, also called a "landing page." This is typically the first page a person sees when visiting your site. No matter where your visitors are on your site, it is important that they always be provided with the "Home" option so they can easily get back to the home page. Nothing is more frustrating than having to click the back arrow several times to get back to the landing page. Your site needs to be easy to navigate, and a "Home" option is key to this ease of navigation.

11. *Use third-party endorsements on your home page.* In my experience, I have learned prospects don't believe what business owners say, since they think that the business owner will say whatever it takes to make a sale. This is why third-party testimonials are so important to grow your business. Prospects will believe your customers before they will believe you. Incorporate these third-party testimonials front and center on your home page, as this is more powerful than any other words you may have on your site. If you do this, I guarantee that you will see an increase in response. The best way to gather testimonials is to ask for them. When you run across customers who have enjoyed your product or service, ask if you can have them send you a brief e-mail summarizing their positive service with your company. Then ask them if you can display this on your site. You will find that almost all will allow you to do so.

12. *Place your photo and video on your site.* People like seeing with whom they do business. However, in Internet marketing,

most all transactions take place between buyer and seller without the two ever meeting. I believe a site with your photo will help customers gain trust in you more quickly than a site with no photograph. It is worth spending a hundred dollars or so to have a professional photo taken of yourself. I also encourage you to place your photo on your business cards. Also, your video will introduce you more easily to your prospects.

13. *Have e-commerce set up to accept credit cards.* With over 162 million web sites online, literally billions of dollars are spent on online purchases via credit cards. If you are in Internet marketing, you need to make it easy for people to buy from you. The best way to make your transaction go smoothly is to get an e-commerce merchant account that will allow you to accept Visa and Master-Card. I recommend ViaKlix at (800) 377-3962 or online at www.ViaKlix.com to get set up. I have used ViaKlix for a number of years and all my web sales revenue is directly deposited into my business checking account. If you sell on eBay, you may not need to get your own e-commerce account, but I would then recommend that you get set up through PayPal at www.PayPal.com.

14. *List your web address on everything.* One of the greatest challenges of owning an Internet marketing business is attracting prospects to your site. I recommend you include your web address on all of your company materials: business cards, letterhead, return address labels, license plate frames, and so forth. I even have a large sign of www.CreateYourOwnDestiny.com in the back window of my car that I can put up and take down as needed. When I am traveling for business, I display my sign, and everyone I pass on the freeway (or who passes me) can see my site address. Additionally, when I park my car in parking lots, I prominently display my sign. Remember, people passing by only have a few moments to glance at it; yet another reason your domain name needs to be short enough to remember with one glance. I have sold many books as a result of my sign and even landed a few speaking engagements as well.

15. *Have a counting device on your site.* A counting device tells you how many "hits" or visits your site gets. If you have a small

counter at the bottom of your site, you will be able to monitor the number of visitors you receive. This is important because you can evaluate which marketing efforts are bringing traffic to your site and which are not working. You may want to hide your counting device so it is only visible to you.

16. *Evaluate which pages are being visited.* Your webmaster can create reports showing which of your web pages are being visited the most. This is important because you can determine how many visitors are actually going to your web store. Once you evaluate these reports, you can decide if you need to make changes to your site.

17. *Ask visitors for feedback.* Feedback from visitors to your web site is extremely important as it gives you a gauge regarding how you are doing. The best way to do this, once you have your "Free Stuff" and "Newsletter Sign-Up" in place on your site, is to have your webmaster set up a system so when people sign up, you get an e-mail alerting you of new subscribers. Reply to these individuals via e-mail to thank them for visiting your site, ask them if you can be of additional service, ask them for feedback on your site, and most importantly, ask how they stumbled across your site in the first place (this may be the best marketing research you can do). When people purchase from your site, make sure you follow up within a week to ensure their satisfaction and ask them for referrals.

18. *Provide "Zoom-In" capability.* Whatever you are selling on your site, it is very important that the buyer be able to easily view your products. To do so, I recommend that you have your site built in a way that they can "zoom-in" on every item you are selling. What I mean is, when they click on the item, a larger image of the product becomes visible on their screen. People like to see exactly what they are buying.

19. *Use a consistent color scheme.* This may be obvious, but I have seen far too many businesses where the web site colors, business cards, and company letterhead do not match. It is important to coordinate all these together so that you have a consistent

look throughout your business. Also, find or develop a company logo that fits your color scheme.

20. *Do not rely solely on search engines for traffic.* I've saved maybe the most important item for last. Many people think that if they get their site listed with a search engine and have a high placement, then they will receive tons of visitors to their site. This may be true, but placement on search engines is a moving target. You may have a high placement today, but this will change on a regular basis. It is important to have a solid search engine placement strategy, but, no matter what you do, it is crucial that this be only *part* of your marketing efforts and not your *only* effort.

All of these web strategies are important and should not be overlooked. You can make it easy on yourself by instructing your webmaster to follow the steps just outlined to ensure your site's success.

If you still need help with this, Stores Online is a solid resource (www.StoresOnline.com) that can also help you build and maintain your web site. They will certainly follow the aforementioned steps to ensure your success and provide you with a complete Internet education.

REAL-LIFE EXAMPLES OF ENTREPRENEURS USING THE INTERNET

On the following pages are the profiles of seven ordinary people with limited or no advanced education or training on the Internet, making money from home using the Internet to market their products and services:

Name and Web Site:	**Tim from California** (www.ProfitPress.com)
Business:	Selling e-books from web store to contractors

(continued)

(*continued*)

Office Location:	From home
Before Launching Business:	Freelance writer and editor
Months to Profitability:	Four
Unique Selling Proposition:	Contractor-friendly information in a concise format
Challenges:	Getting large amounts of traffic to web store
Internet Benefits:	Selling electronic files so there is NO inventory
Hours Worked:	Part-time
Advice to Others:	Partner with someone who knows the Web very well
Monthly Income:	$500 per month (biggest month $2,000)

Name and Web Site:	**Mary from Massachusetts** (www.ToleSampler.com)
Business:	Selling art and custom-painted items on web
Office Location:	From home
Before Launching Business:	Chemistry teacher
Months to Profitability:	12
Unique Selling Proposition:	Customized hand-painted, original artwork
Challenges:	Getting more traffic to web site
Internet Benefits:	Ability to market art to a worldwide market
Hours Worked:	Full-time
Advice to Others:	Must sell something that you are passionate about
Monthly Income:	$1,000 per month (biggest month was $2,500)

Name and Web Site:	**Mike from Montana** (www.eBay.com)

Business:	Selling clothes, CDs, electronics, and artifacts on eBay
Office Location:	From home
Before Launching Business:	Mortgage broker
Months to Profitability:	Two
Unique Selling Proposition:	Has developed a strong track record on eBay for delivering
Challenges:	Finding valuable items for cheap to sell at large profits
Internet Benefits:	Ability to reach buyers all over the world
Hours Worked:	Part time in between other projects
Advice to Others:	Shop at department store close-out sales to maximize profits
Monthly Income:	$850 per month (biggest month was $2,500)
Name and Web Site:	**Thomas from Washington** (www.eBay.com)
Business:	Selling religious and self-help books, CDs, and DVDs
Office Location:	From home
Before Launching Business:	Family crisis counselor
Months to Profitability:	12
Unique Selling Proposition:	Most products are not available elsewhere
Challenges:	Constantly having to search for/ find new inventory
Internet Benefits:	Doesn't have to go to work any longer, freedom
Hours Worked:	Full-time
Advice to Others:	Sell items of familiarity and always keep learning

(continued)

(*continued*)

Monthly Income:	$1,000 per month (biggest month $2,800)
Name and Web Site:	**Lisa from Florida** (www.TShirtsToo.com)
Business:	Selling t-shirts and stickers on the Web (www.StickersEtc.com)
Office Location:	From home
Before Launching Business:	Housewife (husband was laid off so she started business)
Months to Profitability:	Three
Unique Selling Proposition:	No minimum volume requirement on shirts or stickers
Challenges:	Increased competition on the Web
Internet Benefits:	Can market services to the entire world
Hours Worked:	Full-time
Advice to Others:	Focus on getting high search engine placements
Monthly Income:	$1,000 per month (biggest month $20,000)
Name and Web Site:	**Cecilia from Florida** (www.cjbisset.com)
Business:	Selling own paintings (water color and pastels)
Office Location:	From home art studio
Before Launching Business:	Miscellaneous odd jobs
Months to Profitability:	One
Unique Selling Proposition:	Custom paintings that match client decor wishes
Challenges:	Keeping up with inventory; creating more paintings

Internet Benefits:	Conveniently can access global marketplace
Hours Worked:	Full-time
Advice to Others:	Create web site to market paintings and attend art shows
Monthly Income:	$3,000 per month (biggest month $22,000)
Name and Web Site:	**Vickie from California** (www.VickieToy.com)
Business:	Selling stuffed animals and teddy bears on the Web
Office Location:	From office building
Before Launching Business:	Travel agent
Months to Profitability:	Six
Unique Selling Proposition:	Never out of stock; ships product same day order is taken
Challenges:	Competing on price, quality, and style
Internet Benefits:	Ability to market direct to end customers worldwide
Hours Worked:	Full-time (now 10 employees)
Advice to Others:	Focus on search engine placement even though it costs money
Monthly Income:	$170,000 per month (over $2 million per year)

As you can see, these are just regular folks taking advantage of the many benefits the Internet has to offer to produce additional income for their families. These folks work both part-time and full-time and are all marketing something they enjoy from the comfort of their home. However, all of them started part-time. These entrepreneurs are men and women, 25 to 75 years old.

I included the profile of Vickie Toy Factory to show you the unlimited income potential Internet marketing offers. Vickie was an unhappy travel agent in 1995 before launching her company: now she has a team of 10 employees and her company is generating more than $2 million per year in revenues. Whether your goals are to earn an extra $200 per month or $2,000,000 per year, marketing your products and services via the Internet is an ideal way to help you create your own destiny.

If a disgruntled travel agent with no advanced education or Internet training can earn $2 million per year on the Internet selling teddy bears, then I believe virtually anyone, regardless of their age or computer proficiency, can make an extra $500 per month selling something they are passionate about on the Internet.

Getting started in business for yourself can be intimidating if you don't know exactly what you are doing. I encourage you to seek out the assistance of a friend who has successfully launched a business. If you have a difficult time finding such a person, I have identified a couple of companies, such as Stores Online and eBay, that can help you get started marketing your hobbies on the Internet.

Summary

You are now at a point where you have learned the most important things for being successful in business. Now it is time to take action and execute your plan *daily*. Conrad Hilton said:

> "Success seems to be connected with action.
> Successful people keep moving.
> They make mistakes, but they don't quit."[5]

Just because you read a book about weight loss doesn't mean you are going to lose weight. You will only lose weight once you *implement the strategies* covered in the book. The same concept is true in business. Reading this book is not going to ensure that your business will be successful. You must take action, execute your plan, and implement the strategies covered in this chapter.

As you build your business and proceed forward, you are bound to come across obstacles that will overwhelm you at times and even force you to think about giving up. This is only natural. We all at times doubt our abilities. During these times, remember that the key to being successful in life and in business is to simply rise one more time than you fall. If you can commit to doing this, then you are destined to become a successful business owner.

If you have gotten this far in my book, I have no doubt that you will be successful *when* you implement these strategies. I wish you all the success and freedom that a successful business can provide you. America is a great country for many reasons, but I believe our free enterprise system is the best in the world, and it's the primary reason I encourage you to get started in your own business today.

I challenge you to implement all the strategies outlined in this book. Whether you start an Internet marketing business or any kind of business, it is important to note that the ideas, techniques, and strategies offered in this chapter apply to any kind of business that you launch. Regardless of the business you decide to start, make sure it is in line with your passions and always remember: the road to success almost always makes a brief stop at failure. Just because you have tried business ownership in the past and failed, does not mean you can't become a successful entrepreneur. The wealthiest entrepreneurs oftentimes have overcome many failures. If you apply the resources in this chapter to your business, I guarantee you will soar.

CHAPTER 11

Choosing Health, Nutrition, and Exercise Daily

Every man is the builder of a temple called his body.
We are all sculptors and painters, and our material is our
flesh and bones.
—Henry David Thoreau[1]

Do diets work? Have you experienced the ups and downs of
weight loss, and then weight gain, again and again? Are you
frustrated with your weight? Do you wish you could lose those
extra 10 or 25 pounds that have haunted you for years?

Have you tried every diet under the sun only to be disappointed, not having the time, energy, or ability to make custom
meals three times a day (as many of today's diets require us to do)?

If you've struggled with these questions over the years, I want
you to know that you are not alone. I, too, have faced these same
challenges. There's good news, though. I've discovered a solution
that will help you lose weight, get in the best shape of your life, and
have more energy than ever before.

I've included this chapter because I believe it doesn't do you any
good to create and achieve your destiny if your body can't keep up.
Your body is a unique gift. To pursue your passions and achieve your
destiny, being in good health is not just important, it's imperative.

I have written this chapter in a very simple manner. Why?
Because too often, people get overwhelmed with the science

behind the basics, so much so that they don't grasp the principles of proper health and nutrition. Also, if you went to a bookstore's weight-loss and nutrition section, you'd find hundreds of books written on these subjects. I believe there is too much information for most people to assimilate. I created this chapter to help you learn what you need to do to lose weight once and for all and get into the best shape of your life. I am furthermore challenging you to take action on your weight-loss goals by showing you how easy it is to apply my program to your life on a *daily* basis.

DISCLAIMER: I am not a physician, nutritionist, or health specialist of any kind. To ensure your safety, I recommend that you discuss these strategies with your physician prior to starting any new exercise routine or changing your current eating regimen.

The suggestions throughout this chapter are not based on specific scientific research. Rather, the thoughts and ideas presented here are common sense and summarize the basics of what all experts have been talking about for years. All I can tell you is, if you desire to search for the evidence and proof regarding what I'm about to share with you, you won't have to look hard.

These strategies have worked for me. I believe they will work for you too—but only if you apply them daily. The old philosophy is, if you want to be successful, do what successful people have done. If you want to be wealthy, do what wealthy people have done. Weight loss and better nutrition are not rocket science! If you want to be healthy and in better shape, exercise and eat like healthy people do. My program is really that simple. It all comes down to choices that we make every day.

I firmly believe that to be thin, you first must see yourself as being thin.

It's another example of what I've said throughout this book: *those who see the invisible can achieve the impossible.* For some of you, weight loss may appear to be impossible. However, the following guidelines are all you need to lose weight and gain energy. You've heard these over and over again throughout the years. *Now* is the time to apply this information to your situation so that you can transform your life and create your own destiny.

Three Steps to Good Health and Weight Loss

1. Eliminate sweets from your diet.

2. Exercise daily.

3. Drink nothing but water, and lots of it.

That's it! Often, simpler is better, which I believe to be true here. Again, it all comes down to the choices we make each day. I recently chose to live by these three rules, and, as a result, have made extraordinary progress toward achieving my health goals.

Let me tell you my story. During the summer of 2005, I tore the rotator cuff in my shoulder. Because of this injury, I didn't exercise for almost four months. During this time I gained 15 pounds. That's not a whole lot, but I was already 25 pounds heavier than I should have been. Even though my football days had long since passed, I was still eating like I ate as a teenager. Between ages 18 and 36, I slowly gained 55 pounds.

Finally I'd had enough. I made up my mind and chose to do the following to help me achieve my better-health goals: when I began, I woke up every day and read the following,

"I will exercise and eat healthily today!"

And then I did just that. As a result, I slowly lost nearly all the weight that I had gained during the past 18 years and I have more energy than ever before.

Now, I didn't succeed because I had an abundance of spare time. As a parent and hard-working entrepreneur, I almost always chose to spend time with my kids or build my business instead of exercising. Sure, I would exercise now and again. But I certainly didn't stick to any kind of regular routine. As a result,

I became overweight. Now I am becoming thin again. You can do the same.

During those years when I was putting on the pounds, I became an addict. I became addicted to sugar and sweets. Back in my boyhood days, I could put away more cookies than anyone. I never met any cookie dough I didn't like. Candy bars were my midday snacks. I never passed over a single dessert. Finally, when I was at the heaviest weight of my life—242 pounds—I started to suspect that eating an overabundance of sweets was the source of my problem. It seemed as though the more sweets I ate, the more I craved them. This became a vicious cycle, as every night after dinner, I made sure to have a big dessert.

My theory was reinforced by Morgan Spurlock's film, *Super Size Me*. According to Spurlock's findings, food manufacturers have been adding sugar and other additives to many of our foods, which ultimately increases our cravings and gives us a false sense of being hungry. No wonder the United States is suffering from an obesity epidemic. I believe Spurlock's conclusions as to why food manufacturers do this: it all comes down to making more profits. To combat these cravings, I finally started my program and experienced amazing results within the first week.

I followed three rules: eliminate sweets, exercise every day, and drink only water. I challenge you to incorporate these rules into your lifestyle. You will be amazed with the results.

As a result, I've lost a lot of weight and my energy level has skyrocketed. Soon I will be at the weight I was when I graduated from college. What a great feeling! It has been so simple and all I did was follow these three rules daily. Let's look at each of these in more detail.

ELIMINATING SWEETS

When I was addicted to sugar, I thought there would be no way I could eliminate all sweets. You may feel the same way; you don't know if you can give up chocolate or whatever your weakness is. That's why it's important to read this affirmation each morning: *"I choose to eat healthily and exercise today."*

I found that after a week without eating sweets, I no longer desired them. The cravings completely stopped.

Then a funny thing happened to me. Once I stopped eating sweets, my appetite diminished almost immediately, and my weight began to drop noticeably.

Try this for yourself: eat any kind of food you want. Carbs, no carbs, it doesn't matter. Eat your pizza, pasta, and anything else, as long as it doesn't fall into the following categories. Eat whatever big meals you want, just do *not* eat any sweets. By sweets, I mean foods that contain "bad sugar," such as:

- Ice cream
- Cookies
- Doughnuts
- Candy
- Cake
- Pie
- Pudding
- Syrup
- Jam or jelly
- Soft drinks
- Milkshakes
- Junk food
- All juices
- Any kind of dessert

You get the point. Sure, pasta, bread, and other staples contain sugar, but not in such high amounts. Studies show that the kind of sugar in sweets and junk foods boosts your level of insulin, which turns the high-sugar food you've eaten into fat much quicker than foods with less sugar. If this is difficult to understand, let me make it simple for you:

Bad sugar makes you fat.

I know what you may be thinking—how do I deal with my sugar cravings when they hit? Do what I have done and replace "bad" sugar with "good" sugar. What is "good sugar"? This is the natural sugar found in fruit. Replace sweets with fruits and good things will happen. I don't mean canned fruit, since canned fruit is usually packed in syrup. I mean natural whole fruits (organic if possible): apples, oranges, pears, bananas, and so forth.

Good sugar gives you energy.

If you cut out sweets and junk food, your grocery bill will drop along with your weight. Fruit is more economical than candy. Organic fruit is a little more expensive, but I definitely think it's worth the price to keep you healthier in the long run.

EXERCISE

What sweets are your weaknesses? What fruits do you like that you can enjoy instead?

_____

_____

_____

EXERCISING DAILY

Old studies said that, for optimal health, you should do 20 minutes of cardiovascular exercise three times a week. Good idea, but I don't think you will lose any weight following that routine. I believe, to lose weight, you must exercise much more.

My program calls for a minimum of 60 minutes of exercise every single day, seven days a week, 365 days per year. This may seem extreme, but if you want to lose weight, this is a must.

Studies show that exercise reduces depression and strengthens your heart, bones, and muscles. Daily exercise gives you more energy to accomplish more things. And daily exercise does a very good job burning off the food you eat, which helps with your weight-loss goals.

I know what you may be thinking: how in the world am I going to find time in my day to exercise, given my crazy schedule? It's simple, really: treat daily exercise the same as you would a meeting with an important client. If you were going to meet an important client, you would schedule that time into your day.

I recommend that you add daily exercise to your calendar. As a result, you will *make* time to exercise, and you'll benefit tremendously.

After exercising for 30 days, you'll find that your body will crave exercise. It's a natural "release" and stress reliever. You will soon discover that you're a better person, better parent, and better entrepreneur as a result of your daily exercise.

The next question you may be asking yourself is: what kind of exercise is the best for me? I believe it's important to mix it up so that you don't get tired of doing the same thing over and over again.

One exercise I recommend is walking. It's low-impact, so it's not bad for your back or knees. Virtually anyone can do it, and it's a great way to get fresh air. I suggest that you find three or four exercise "passions" and build them into your daily routine.

I enjoy walking with my wife, walking along the beach with my dogs, mountain biking with my kids, and going to the gym to work out. I try my best to mix these up, so I won't tire of doing the same one or two things over and over again.

EXERCISE

What are three different kinds of exercise that you enjoy that you can start doing every day?

_____

_____

_____

DRINKING WATER

Many of us have grown so accustomed to drinking diet sodas, coffee, and juice that we've lost a sense of what we really want when we're thirsty: water. Without question, water is the *best* drink for you, as it rehydrates your cells, replenishes you when you sweat, and is all natural, with nothing at all unhealthy for you.

The best thing about water is that it has zero calories, so you can drink as much as you like. The more water you drink, the more it cleanses your body of the harmful toxins that we all take in every day.

Water helps with digestion. It's good for your colon, your skin, your blood, your hair, your kidneys, your liver, and your brain. I rarely get headaches, but when I do, drinking lots of water makes my headaches go away. Drink a lot of water the next time you get a headache and I think you'll be surprised with the results. Your body benefits from water in countless ways.

According to a recent University of Washington medical study, a new formula was discovered to determine just how much water you should drink daily. Take your weight and divide this number by two. If you live in a dry climate add 10 percent. This figure equals the number of recommended ounces of water to drink daily.

The way I look at it, if I want to eat more food, I need to eliminate any calories I get from liquids. Your body does not need any other kind of liquid but water. All other drinks are manufactured and marketed for the sake of making a profit—but you don't actually need any of them. Try rice milk for your breakfast cereal.

In interviewing health and reverse aging expert, Joan Bunney, author of *Sexy in Your 60's*, I learned the importance of drinking acid-free alkaline water. Not only is it a good idea to drink nothing but water, but it is an even better idea to drink water that contains a high pH factor. According to Joan, the great alkaline reserve is the body's bank account. A substance is either alkaline or acid, based on its pH (potential Hydrogen). The correct pH balance largely determines your body's overall wellness. The level of acidity in your body is determined by your diet and other factors. As the body accumulates acidic waste, these acidic products will often result in disease. Acid-free alkaline water neutralizes harmful acids, disposes of them safely, and lowers the acidity of the body's pH, resulting in high immunity against disease, and reverses the aging process on all levels. Many experts in this area of study (including Joan) believe that it is very difficult to get cancer if your body has low acidity—proper pH balance. Drink lots of acid-free alkaline water and you will experience better *health* as a result. You may also be able to slow the aging process.

If you don't believe me, I encourage you to read one of the many books on this topic. My two favorites are by medical doctor Fereydoon Batmanghelidj: *You're Not Sick, You're Thirsty* and *Your Body's Many Cries for Water*. In both books, Dr. Batmanghelidj lists 46 reasons why your body needs plenty of water every day. He concludes that numerous diseases can be prevented by drinking adequate amounts of water on a daily basis. I highly recommend both books if you want to better understand why water is one of nature's best cures. Two other enlightening books I recommend are *Reverse Aging*, by Sang Whang, and *Alkalize or Die*, by Dr. Theodore A. Baroody.

If you are looking for a way to insure that you can access high pH water, I would highly recommend that you purchase a water ionizer that produces Kangen Water from Enagic USA. To learn more about this great company and their water ionizers, visit them on the web at www.Enagic.com or call (310) 542-7700 to find a distributor near you.

Let's look at some of the negative things about beverages other than water.

- Coffee: loaded with caffeine, which is addictive
- Soft drinks: loaded with eight to twelve teaspoons of sugar, full of caffeine and calories
- Diet soft drinks: loaded with man-made chemicals
- Juice: loaded with sugar (but at least not caffeine)
- Milk: if not organic, includes growth hormones
- Beer, wine, liquor: addictive, impairs motor skills, lots of calories
- Tea: can be good for you, but not as good as pure water

All of these beverages are popular. But I challenge you to choose water over these drinks. If you do, you'll lose weight and gain energy.

EXERCISE

List your top beverages of choice below. Now, go a week drinking only water. Come back later and describe your results.

_____

_____

_____

STRATEGIES FOR WEIGHT LOSS AND HEALTHY EATING

Don't forget: it can take a lot of time to get back to your desired weight. Just as your body slowly added the extra weight, it will slowly come off. Avoid unrealistic expectations, such as losing 30 pounds in 30 days. I think a pound a week is more realistic and long lasting. If your goal is to lose 50 pounds, give yourself 50 weeks, or a year, and I believe that your weight will come off and stay off. Also, to keep a positive attitude about the process, only weigh yourself twice a month. If you do this, each time you get on the scale, you will usually be one to two pounds lighter than you were on the previous weigh-in.

Here are 15 things you can do to improve your health, reduce your weight, and help you gain more energy:

1. Eliminate sweets altogether.

2. Exercise daily.

3. Drink lots of water.

4. Eat lots of fruits and vegetables.

5. Avoid alcohol, tobacco, and drugs.

6. Get eight hours of sleep nightly.

7. Eat a high-fiber diet or take fiber supplements.

8. Get plenty of sunshine and fresh air.

9. Eat four to five half-meals per day.

10. Always eat breakfast.

11. Eat whole natural almonds as snacks.

12. Avoid eating after 7 PM.

13. Drink a glass of water before every meal.

14. Supplement your diet with vitamins and calcium.

15. Try eliminating red meat from your diet.

A SPECIAL NOTE

I have read numerous books on nutrition and have come to learn about the connection between heart disease and a diet high in red meat. I have also learned that red meat is a very acidic food that is difficult for your body to digest. Additionally, I've learned that a high acidic diet (consisting of lots of sugar and red meat) provides a good environment for cancer to grow. I highly encourage you to read *Beyond the 120 Year Diet* by Roy Walford. As a result of these findings, I have eliminated all red meat from my diet and have lost weight and seen my waistline shrink significantly. Try it yourself for 30 days; you will be amazed with the results!

SUMMARY

Most of us enter the workforce around age 20, in good health, and then spend the next 30 years working to earn money, only to lose our health in the process. Once our health is lost (as a result of working for 30 years), we spend all the money we've earned to try to regain the health of our youth. Eventually, we end up as 80-year-olds with neither our health nor our wealth. This is *not* my goal for you. I want you to achieve more *health* and the best way to do this is by taking *massive* actions in your life.

Thinking about weight loss and actually losing weight are two different things. Reading diet books and joining health clubs or purchasing exercise equipment will *not* help you lose weight and achieve your goals. These acts are not enough. You must follow the advice of nutritional experts and actually go to the gym and exercise on a regular basis to achieve your goals. It all comes down to making good choices on a daily basis, over several months, until real transformation has occurred.

Your choices define you. As philosopher John Dewey said,

"The self is not something ready made, but something in continuous formation through choice of action."[2]

If you want to lose weight and get in the best shape of your life, you must first choose to do so, then apply your plan over and over again on a daily basis for months and months to achieve the results you desire. What I have offered in this chapter is *one* of many ways to lose weight and gain energy. It has worked for me, and I believe it will work for you. Remember, it's always important to consult with your physician.

Finally, it takes a long time to gain weight, so give yourself an adequate amount of time to lose the weight as well. I promise you that if you stick to this plan, over time, and make good choices on a daily basis, you will experience a new you. You will make the transformation, begin a new way of life, and show the world the real you.

Don't put off for another day what you can start immediately. Promise yourself that you will indeed *choose to eat healthily and exercise today!* Achieve the desired weight and level of health that you want. My promise to you is that, if you apply the basics of this chapter, you will indeed experience more *health* in life.

If you incorporate the ideas in this chapter in your life on a daily basis, I am very confident that you will also experience more *happiness* in your life.

CHAPTER 12

Making Permanent Changes in Your Life

Formal education will make you a living; self-education
will make you a fortune.
—Jim Rohn[1]

What's next? You are almost finished with this book and
perhaps riding on cloud nine, now believing that all things
are possible. You may be feeling a boost in motivation.

But beware—this feeling is probably only a temporary high.
Temporary change is *not* what I want for you. My goal is to help
you make real-life *permanent* changes to benefit you for the rest of
your life.

MOTIVATION VERSUS INSPIRATION

It has never been my goal simply to make money as a
motivational speaker and author. Rather, my goal is to be an
inspirational speaker and author, one who helps my audiences
and readers transform themselves on a permanent basis into the
kind of people they want to become. Let me explain.

Too often motivation becomes like a temporary high—something that lifts us up for a short time, perhaps an hour or two, or
maybe even a couple of days. Once this passes, we usually come
crashing down off the high and revert right back to our old habits
and thoughts, which, many times, hinder our actions. As a result, in
the end we are no better off.

Only you can truly change yourself; only you can generate permanent motivation for yourself.

My goal is not to motivate you in order to change you right away. My goal is to inspire you to make changes in yourself—changes that you are capable of; changes you want to make.

When you complete this book, I want to have given you resources and strategies to help you make these internal changes. Often we need ongoing coaching and ongoing continuing education and, most importantly, ongoing inspiration, to ensure that these transformations take hold and change our lives permanently.

I want you to know that I share your pain as well as your joys in this journey. When I began writing this book in 1996, I was broke. I was struggling financially, with virtually nothing to show for my years of hard work on the job. I was out of shape and completely discontented with my life. All I had was determination to make real-life changes and a drive to help others do the same. Well, today, more than 14 years later, I have retired from corporate America, I'm free of consumer loans, and I'm making more money as a business owner than ever before—all because of this transformation that I am talking about. You, too, can experience real-life change in your life if you take action daily, follow the recommendations I've given in this book, hire a coach as an accountability partner, and most importantly, surround yourself with positive people and life-changing ideas on a regular basis.

I have created a way to help you experience transformation on a permanent basis. Like other long-term solutions, this will require an investment of both time and money. Always remember:

The best investment you can make is an investment in yourself.

I embrace this maxim of Benjamin Franklin's:

"If a man empties his purse in his head, no one can take it away from him.
An investment in knowledge always pays the best interest."[2]

DESTINY COACH NETWORK

Coaching is one of the best ways to ensure that you will achieve your life's goals. Having a coach to serve as an "accountability partner" gives you the ability to speak with someone in confidence on a regular basis. A coach provides that extra kick in the pants we sometimes need to continue pursuing our goals—even when all the odds seem to be against us.

I created the Destiny Coach Network for your benefit. I am unable to keep up with all the personal coaching requests I receive, so I have built a large network of life coaches. If you're interested in the Destiny Coach Network, visit my web site for a list of coaches. Choose a coach from that list, and I'll set up a complimentary 30-minute consultation for you. This is your chance to see which coach would be the best match for you. I am passionate about connecting people to a coach who fits their interests and outlooks, one who can help you make permanent changes in your life.

If your budget does not allow you to hire a coach and you are looking to earn extra income, then a different approach might suit you better. For this reason I encourage you to join iLearningGlobal.

ILEARNINGGLOBAL.TV

iLearningGlobal (ILG) offers a personal development library for entrepreneurs, salespeople, small-business owners, lifelong learners, and other professionals. It's an exciting new organization that promises to forever change the way we learn.

iLearningGlobal leverages full-screen high-definition video streaming technology by providing its members a portal to learning. This subscription-based library of knowledge provides access to the world's best minds and ideas in the field of personal growth and development. iLearningGlobal is already on its way to becoming the world's largest e-learning, continuing education, and webucation organization.

iLearningGlobal leverages the street smarts, global experience, and intellectual property of the best authors, speakers, coaches, and consultants of our time in sales, marketing, management, leadership, entrepreneurship, tax and investment strategies, parenting, relationships, negotiating, and many other areas. Content is delivered via the latest technology through e-books, audio books, and video to your PC, laptop, or mobile device.

ILEARNINGGLOBAL FACULTY

iLearningGlobal offers content from the most successful experts in the world, including the following:

Brian Tracy, Tony Alessandra, Sandy Botkin, Omar Periu, Jim Britt, Don Hutson, Kevin Carroll, Dan Clark, Dolf de Roos, Scott Michael Zimmerman, Mark Victor Hansen, Bob Proctor, John Gray, Patricia Fripp, Dennis Deaton, Paul Martinelli, Terri Murphy, Dave Sherman, Tom Ferry, Allan Pease, Harv Eker, Jim Cathcart, Leslie Householder, Steve Anderson, Garrett Gunderson, Chet Holmes, Shep Hyken, Tom Feltenstein, Ivan Misner, Dawn Billings, Marsha Petrie Sue, Bill Bartmann, Tom Hinton, Hyrum Smith, Patrick Snow, TJ Hoisington, Debbie Allen, Paula Fellingham, Marcia Brixey, Ron Finklestein, Joe Newman, Don Mastrangelo, Darol Wagstaff, Kim Power Stilson, Mark Papadas, Greg Baer, Jesse Ferrell, Terri Dunevant, Steve Siebold, Wendy Patton, Victor Antonio G., and more.

In the months and years ahead, we will add more of the world's best to our team. If you have an interest in becoming a member of iLearningGlobal or becoming a faculty member, please get in touch with the person who recommended this book or gave you a copy.

iLearningGlobal Mission

As both an iLearningGlobal founding member and faculty presenter, I am proud to share more about the organization and its three primary goals:

1. To make you a better person.

2. To provide you with an additional stream of income.

3. To provide a mastermind learning environment.

As Jim Rohn said at the beginning of this chapter, "Self-education will make you a fortune." Our goal with ILG is to help you become a better mother, father, spouse, employee, employer—a better person. We want to help you become a better salesperson, a better entrepreneur, a better small-business owner, and more. Whatever you do in life, we want to make you better at it. We want to help you achieve all your goals faster and better than you would otherwise. In essence, we want to help you become better than you were before through the e-learning resources provided by iLearningGlobal.

If you have a direct sales organization, you might think at first glance that ILG poses a threat to your business. The opposite is true. We designed ILG to help your existing direct sales company grow even faster. Studies tell us that roughly 80 percent of people who go into the direct selling industry eventually leave the business. At ILG, our goal is to provide these folks with the resources to stay in the industry and, beyond that, become more successful! We believe that the majority of ILG's Mastermind members are building other direct selling companies, and we believe our webucation offerings will make them even more successful in building these new companies.

Mastermind Marketing

We'll talk more about the powerful results of being part of a mastermind group in the next chapter. However, in this section,

I want to briefly introduce a concept known as "Mastermind Marketing." It's designed to help you achieve the aforementioned number two mission: "creating an additional stream of income."

Masterminding can be traced back at least 100 years to when Andrew Carnegie enlisted the help of Napoleon Hill in interviewing some of the greatest entrepreneurs and business leaders of the day.

What's important is that a mastermind group is only as good as the people involved and the information communicated amongst the group members. With this in mind, ILG gives you access to our family of masterminds, which already stands at 60 of the world's greatest experts in their fields—and that number is growing!

Through ILG, you can make permanent changes in your life. You'll immerse yourself in our mastermind group and increase your level of knowledge and personal growth. Through your membership in iLearningGlobal, you'll have access to quarterly mastermind conferences, monthly mastermind group sessions, and daily faculty calls. Additionally, if you refer others to become part of this new way of learning, you'll receive commissions through our mastermind marketing plan.

For more information about the ILG commission plan, joining a mastermind group, and the webucation industry that is predicted to be "an industry worth hundreds of billions of dollars in the future" (Peter Drucker, quoted in *Forbes* magazine), contact the person who gave you this book, or visit www.OutEarnYour Bills.com and www.iLearningGlobal.tv.

SELF-LIMITING BELIEFS

One of the greatest challenges we face when attempting to create and achieve our destiny is changing our self-limiting beliefs. These beliefs, developed over years and years, hold us back from getting all that we want out of life. One of the major goals of iLearningGlobal is to help you change these limiting beliefs, set you free, and allow you to experience a personal transformation that will allow you to get *more* out of life.

As world-renowned motivational speaker and best-selling author Anthony Robbins said,

> "Your past does not equal your future!"[3]

If you can remember this as you reflect on your past and plan for your future, you will realize that it is only your belief system that holds you back from creating your own destiny. As you read this book and join iLearningGlobal, you will realize you are indeed a new you.

The self-limiting rules that previously applied to your thinking and behavior no longer exist. Unforeseen circumstances and a new belief system will come to your aid to give you the will to create and achieve your destiny.

As you implement the strategies in the previous chapter of choosing to exercise and eat healthily, you are slowly transforming your body day by day. You are indeed a new and better you. Your future is bright. You can and will get what you want—but only when you eliminate your old self-limiting beliefs.

LIVING YOUR DREAMS

Have you ever wondered what it would feel like to live your dreams? What do you dream about as you sit there, plodding away at your miserable job? How do you want things to be? If you knew you could not fail, what would you pursue? These are tough questions, but also exciting, when you decide to take action and pursue your dreams.

Let me tell you the story of a man who was unhappy at work and changed as a result of investing in self-education. Norm Thomson worked in construction for years. Although he was proud of his work, he was never really satisfied with what he had accomplished in his life. He had big dreams but never took action on those dreams. Over time, Norm made some big changes, which included real estate investing part-time on the side. After a short while, he became so successful at flipping houses that he soon retired from construction. Shortly thereafter, he realized that his true passions were yachting and traveling the South Pacific.

Norm and his wife bought a 46-foot Nordhavn yacht and spent several weeks traveling from Seattle down the West Coast of the United States. They stopped at many ports along the way. Finally, after spending some time in Dana Point, California, he set course for Hawaii. He sailed for 15 days, battling 20-foot waves for two days straight. His experience shows that sometimes you have to fight like mad to get what you desire. Norm took his real estate investing business to a higher level throughout Hawaii.

When we last spoke, he told me he couldn't remember the last time he wore dress shoes or long pants. Now that he knows what it's like to live his dreams, Norm is writing a book to help other people fully live their dreams. His book is titled *Making Your Dreams a Reality*.

Again, I ask you, if you knew you could not fail, what would you pursue? What is holding you back from pursuing your passions *now*?

EXERCISE

List your current self-limiting beliefs:

_____

_____

_____

_____

_____

What permanent changes are you going to make in your life?

_____

_____

_____

_____

_____

Summary

It is my belief that you are the only one who can make real and lasting changes in your life. My goal in writing this book is not to simply motivate you, because I believe that motivation is only temporary. My goal is to inspire you to make lifelong changes that can indeed help you achieve your destiny.

If you need assistance making these changes, I encourage you to become a member by enrolling in iLearningGlobal so you can benefit from all the webucation offered on this site.

I also challenge you to complete the exercises in this chapter. As you do so, you will become free to pursue your passions and live your dreams; you will realize that the only force that can hold you back from getting all you really want is your mind and your self-limiting beliefs. You are capable of more than you think. I believe in you, even if you're at a point where you no longer believe in yourself. You are stronger than you realize and your will is capable of lifting you above your current circumstances to get everything that you desire.

SECTION FOUR

SOAR

❧

More gold has been mined from the
brains of men than has ever been
taken from the earth.
—Napoleon Hill[1]

CHAPTER 13

Leading and Leveraging Your Network

A man's friendships are one of the best
measures of his worth.
—Charles Darwin[2]

If you want more *money* in your life, you must not only count on your own income-earning abilities, but also the abilities of those in your network. You must become the leader in your life and in your family. You must be willing to learn from other leaders and put these financial life lessons to work in your life.

If you want to achieve your biggest dreams, then you must tell people about your dreams. As a result, sooner or later, someone will show up in your life and help make your dreams come true (as discussed at the end of Chapter 1).

It is important to understand that it all comes down to becoming a leader and establishing strong relationships. In order to establish strong relationships, you must identify several areas in your life that you can work on to fully create your own destiny and soar.

These areas might include creating or joining mastermind groups and joint venture partnerships with mentors, coaches, or others in your network. Strong leaders join mastermind groups and also start their own. Let your network leverage you and your skill set to help them attain their dreams as you do the same by leveraging those within your network.

MASTERMIND GROUPS

How many times have you wanted to achieve a certain goal, create a new product or service, or had a major financial problem and you had no one to turn to discuss these issues? If this has happened to you, then you can benefit from a mastermind group. Let me tell you a story.

Believe it or not, in 1927 there were more than 250 automobile manufacturers in the United States. Most of these were very small and were operating in barns or garages. Today, in comparison, there are really only three U.S. auto makers and a handful from Europe, Japan, and South Korea that manufacture automobiles worldwide.

It was during the 1920s that a little-known automobile company named Ford Motor Company was also trying to make a go of it and be the first manufacturer to mass produce the automobile. The company's founder, Henry Ford, did not have the capital required to fund such an aggressive goal of creating an assembly plant capable of mass production.

If it were not for his mastermind group, he would have been stuck and Ford Motor Company would not be what it is today. However, he took his dilemma to the members of his mastermind group, which included Thomas Edison and Harvey Firestone (Firestone Tires). As a result of Ford sharing his dilemma with the group, Harvey Firestone came up with an idea.

Firestone's idea was for Ford to presell his automobiles by collecting $600 per vehicle in advance sales. Ford executed this idea, selling an estimated 375,000 automobiles. As a result, Ford Motor Company raised $225 million in advance sales and then used this money to manufacture the presold automobiles.

This automotive dynasty's success all stemmed from a mastermind group. Do you want to truly soar in life and create your own destiny? Then I challenge you to join or create a mastermind group if you are not already in one.

If you want something you have never had before, you must do something that you have never done before.

EXERCISE

List five of the most talented entrepreneurs that you know. Contact them and create your own mastermind group.

_____

_____

_____

_____

_____

Studies have shown that you will earn the average amount of the five people with whom you spend the most time. If your five best friends are jobless and bankrupt, then there is good chance you will meet the same fate. However, if your five best friends are millionaires, then chances are, you will sooner or later become a millionaire.

JOINT VENTURES

Almost any new business endeavor a person attempts will require some capital (i.e., cash). Joint ventures are potentially profitable moneymaking endeavors for those who need start-up capital. The understanding required for entering joint ventures (JV) is fairly simple. In short, a JV dealmaker acts as a middleman putting two parties together, then earns a share of the newfound profits when both parties benefit from the new arrangement.

Joint ventures can also be structured within a person's existing job. An employee makes arrangements with his or her employer to allow the employee to uncover hidden profits within the business in exchange for a percentage of the newfound profits. One of the best ways to engineer joint ventures is to take strategies that are working successfully in one industry and introduce them to another industry.

It is not *what* you know, but *who* you know. Joint ventures are one of the best ways to create tremendous income for your business.

You can literally start with zero money. People who understand the power of JV deal-making can be stripped of all their clothes, money, wallet, and contacts, and put cash in their pockets within hours. Well, maybe you might need some clothes! You can get the biggest bang for your buck and time with JV deal-making. There are no limits. There can be residual income. Some individuals have made hundreds of millions with joint ventures. The majority of income from *Fortune* 500 corporations comes from joint ventures.

Here are three simple examples of joint venture deal-making that you can put to use without the need for any capital (i.e., cold hard cash):

1. You do some research on the subject of creative marketing referral programs. After you discover a few that you really like, you go to a company and make the following proposition: "Ms. Business Owner, I have an irresistible proposition for you. I have some unique referral programs that can dramatically increase your sales. Here is what I propose: you and I determine what your current sales levels are. Then, we test my three different referral programs. Once we discover which one works best for your business, you pay me 20 percent of the increase in sales revenue that results from my referral method for as long as you use it."

2. You make contact with several self-published authors who have published books on successful selling tactics. Acting as a middleman, you make arrangements to market each other's respective books to each other's mailing lists, earning a percentage of all sales made.

3. Mortgage Company A only does "A credit loans." You act as a middleman to have Company A send their poor credit clients to Company B, who specializes in these loans, for a referral fee (laws permitting).

My vice president of business development and I have put together a unique "one of a kind" joint venture affiliate program where you can have your own free Internet business by working with us as JV partners. Our program is focused on personal growth, business ownership, and money-making strategies with potentially lucrative affiliate referral fees and ongoing residual income.

If you have always wanted your own home-based business, then become our Joint Venture Destiny Partner. To become a Joint Venture Partner, e-mail my Vice President of Business Development, Michael Helgeson, at info@CreateYourOwnDestiny.com.

Surrounding Yourself with Greatness

One way to leverage your network is to seek out mentors who can help you open doors and show you the way. The world is full of mentors who want to help you achieve your destiny. Look for them, these people are all around you, looking to share their insights, knowledge, and experience with you.

A key distinction between a mentor and a coach is that a coach is someone you pay to help you achieve your goals. Mentors help you from the bottom of their hearts, with no intention of ever being paid.

One of my greatest mentors is Brian Tracy, who is the best-selling author of 46 books that have sold more than 42 million copies worldwide. My favorite Brian Tracy book is *Many Miles to Go*. He is considered by many as the world's leading sales trainer and expert in the field of sales, marketing, management, and entrepreneurship. As a result of Brian Tracy's mentoring, I have learned one of the greatest lessons in the world about success—that we need to study the successes and failures of other people. Mr.

Tracy believes that there simply is not enough time in our lives to learn everything we need to know through our own life's experiences. We can reduce our learning curve dramatically if we can take the best knowledge and experience from all of the world's experts who have already experienced many of the same life challenges.

Brian Tracy's experiences remind me of the single most important skill that all successful salespeople and entrepreneurs have mastered. This lesson is the importance of not taking rejection personally, and to continue moving forward with other prospects, even when people tell you "no." Let's face it, some people will buy from you (or join your network) and some people won't buy from you (or won't join your network). So what? Other prospects are waiting. Remember this formula and apply it to all aspects of your life:

$SW4 = Some will, some won't, so what next, someone else is waiting.$

My mentor lives by this motto and so must you if you want to achieve high levels of success and achieve your destiny. I have successfully built my business on this belief. I was able to develop this belief system as a 13-year-old kid in Michigan selling *Detroit Free Press* subscriptions door-to-door back in 1983.

The key reason to have a mentor is to leverage, not only the knowledge of your mentor, but also your mentor's network. Brian Tracy has introduced me to some incredible people, and I continue to benefit as a result. I challenge you to seek out mentors and to be a mentor as well.

THE DESTINY ACHIEVERS CLUB

Are you struggling financially? Have you evaluated dozens of business opportunities and still don't know which to select? If so, perhaps part of the problem is that you are trying to select only one opportunity when you should pursue several opportunities simultaneously.

The mission of the Destiny Achievers Club is to provide you with a personal development library, mastermind groups, wealth creation strategies, and residual income to allow you to experience true freedom through business ownership. This club is designed to forever help you out-earn your bills and create your own destiny!

In order to be successful and create your own destiny, the most important challenge is to find a proven vehicle (or vehicles) that you can execute over time to achieve your destiny. Many of my clients have been very successful in selecting the right vehicle to help them achieve their goals. For those who are still searching, I created the Destiny Achievers Club to help members realize their visions and get exactly what they want out of their lives.

Over the last 20 years, I have researched direct selling from every angle. I have purchased products and services, and even built organizations of over 10,000 people in short periods of time. Additionally, during this time, I spent 15 years in outside corporate sales while moonlighting in the speaking business. After I was laid off again in 2002, I risked every asset that I had and even assets that I did not have to build my business to where it is today.

The Destiny Achievers Club is the result of everything I have worked so hard for over the last 20 years. I believe this club can be that financial vehicle for you that will give you: more *time*, more *money*, more *freedom*, more *health*, more *love*, and more *happiness* in life. Let me explain how the model has evolved up to this point.

While traveling all over North America on a regular basis as an author and keynote speaker, I think I have been recruited perhaps more than anyone else on the planet. Sometimes I have been prospected as many as 18 times in one week by people representing different companies.

I have been amazed and sometimes entertained by this attention, but what shocks me most is that many of these people are convinced their business model is the *only* way to make it. I believe this is not the case. I often see many of these people spending more time bad-mouthing their competition rather than building their own companies. I think there are a million ways to make a million dollars. It just takes the proper execution of one way to achieve this financial goal. The Destiny Achievers Club is only one way to achieve this goal. You and I both know there are many, many other ways.

So, let me explain why tens of thousands of other people just like you believe that the Destiny Achievers Club is not only a way to make lots of money, but a very good way to realize your goals. The "old school" way of thinking teaches you to select only one stream of income and dedicate your life to that one source. This mentality is based on the belief that you pick just one stream of income, then hope and pray that it survives over the long term. I believe that is too risky and does not work.

Consider how this risky model can blind you from advancements in technology, trends in the marketplace, and multiple needs of all consumers for more than just one product or service. The old school teaches us to ride one horse and hope and pray that this one horse takes us to the promised land.

Let's say you won the lottery and were immediately awarded 10 million dollars. If you were to take this money to any financial advisor, the first thing that person would recommend you do is diversify your money in several different kinds of investments such as stocks, bonds, mutual funds, annuities, real estate, and others. In doing so, your level of risk is greatly reduced.

What we offer in the Destiny Achievers Club is a better model. That model is to attach *your* horse to *your* carriage (which happens to hold your family), then look for other proven horses, rein them in and attach these horses to your carriage, too. Secure up to a dozen different horses to your carriage and you will arrive at your destination more quickly than you would with just one horse.

In the fall of 2008, I was introduced to iLearningGlobal and as a result I have joined as a member and the knowledge learned has helped me better diversify my business under The Snow Group umbrella.

We can talk about diversification of your business, but I challenge you to actually take action and make it happen. This reminds me of what Harvey Mackay said:

"Ideas without actions are worthless"[3]

The only way you will be successful as a Destiny Achievers Club member is to *take action* on a daily basis. I am convinced that if you follow the leadership provided by the Destiny Achievers Club, you will realize your destiny and secure your financial future.

To learn more about the Destiny Achievers Club, visit my web site at www.CreateYourOwnDestiny.com and select "Biz Opportunity," or you can visit this site directly by entering www.DestinyAchieversClub.com in your Internet browser.

The most important thing to consider is that I am leveraging my network with the Destiny Achievers Club. I challenge you to do the same. Become a leader and leverage your network so you can secure your financial future. If you feel it is not right to leverage your network, and think having a job is a better alternative, remember that every day when you punch the time clock, your boss, the company owners, and shareholders leverage your time, talent, education, experience, and ability day after day, year after year. In life you are either being leveraged, or you leverage. Either way time will pass, so why not get paid for helping others make money and multiply your efforts instead of relying solely on your own efforts?

EXERCISE

What ways can you diversify your business model to create additional streams of revenue?

Start doing your due diligence to see how you can create additional revenue streams by diversifying your income.

BUSINESS COACHES

Have you ever wondered what you could do to double your personal income without having to work twice as much? I too have desired this result for years, and it took finding the right coach for this to happen in my business. Just as I coach people all over the world, I too have a coach. In fact, I have many coaches whose expertise I have leveraged in order to grow my business. One of my favorite coaches is Dennis Sutter, a very successful real estate coach. He helps real estate agents all over the world double their personal income. In fact, his system helps virtually any entrepreneur double their income without having to spend any more hours working on their business.

In one of our early coaching sessions, I was telling Dennis of my concern about being spread too thin and being pulled in all directions. Let's face it, many small business owners often feel this way. I told him that I am the CEO of my company but also the janitor. I am the VP of sales, as well as the director of administration, billing, accounting, and accounts receivable.

The challenge of wearing so many hats, according to Dennis, is that, in doing so many different tasks, our prospecting hours are reduced dramatically or, in some cases, eliminated altogether. He believes it is all a matter of putting time into prospecting and sooner or later you will get the business. You will have so many prospects that some of them will always come your way. Dennis emphasizes the importance of being the VP of sales for your company a minimum of four hours every day (if you are full-time). If you are part-time, and only working your business two hours per day, make sure that at least one hour of your day is spent prospecting.

I have implemented these strategies with my business and I am now earning almost two times what I was earning before implementing Dennis Sutter's strategy. I have leveraged his knowledge, expertise, and experience. Now, I experience two times the revenue in my business. Dennis Sutter has several other strategies that he gladly shares with his clients. If you are serious about doubling your income and want to hire Dennis Sutter as your coach, send me an e-mail and I will put you in touch with him. He does not have a web site since all of his clients come by way of word-of-mouth.

EXERCISE

What changes can you make in your daily schedule to ensure that you spend a minimum of four hours every day prospecting?

_____

_____

_____

_____

_____

LOCAL NETWORKING CLUBS

How many networking clubs have you joined? I am hopeful that the answer to this question is at least one networking club. The goal of these networking clubs is to leverage each other's network and provide leads for others. As you share leads, they will share leads with you. Often, networking clubs meet once per week early in the morning or at lunchtime. If you are not taking advantage of these clubs, you are losing money for your business.

Friends buy from friends. People buy from those they like. If you want to make more sales, make more friends.

Networking groups are some of the best places to meet new friends, nurture these relationships, and turn them into potential customers for your business. There are many different kinds of networking clubs all over the world. Find a club you like, join it, and then get involved.

Search the Internet and you will find many options. Some of these include Biz Builders (www.BizBuildersUSA.org), LeTip International (www.LeTip.com), and Business Networking International (www.BNI.com). All of these clubs have small fees that keep the organizations growing. When you obtain your first referral, you will earn this fee back tenfold.

When you're a part of a networking club your first goal should be to provide leads and the second goal should be to receive leads. In a sense, you are leveraging your network to offer leads, and, in return, the group is leveraging its network to give you leads back. By all means, no one is losing in this scenario. Being a part of a networking club is truly win-win. This reminds me of what Frank Crane said:

"Use friendliness, but do not use your friends."[4]

GLOBAL NETWORKING ON THE INTERNET

In recent years, the Internet has exploded onto the scene, as evidenced by the numbers discussed in Chapter 10. To drive home this point further, I interviewed a good friend who is an entrepreneur, and global networking guru. Anne Alberg openly discusses the role that online business networking plays in today's business world. This phenomenon is occurring both in the corporate world and for entrepreneurs locally as well as globally.

According to Anne, as globalization continues, people today cannot rely solely on the old-school way of networking in person. With our busy schedules, people today may choose not to attend traditional networking events as they did in the past. Online business networking can provide a new way to meet people with whom you normally would not interact. Anne talks about the importance of getting involved in online business network communities. The three most popular are www.Facebook.com, www.Twitter.com, and www.LinkedIn.com and others include www.MySpace.com, www.FastPitchNetworking.com, www.Direct Matches.com, www.BizNik.com, and numerous others. If you are as overwhelmed by social networking as are many people, at a minimum join and build profiles on the three most popular sites.

While it may have been true years ago, some of these networks started as dating sites and a place to make new friends. Recently many have evolved into a major platform for business-people to generate referrals, market their products and services, collaborate on projects, and to meet other like-minded professionals. There are now over 500 online business networking communities, and new communities are coming online daily. By the time you read this book, there will be thousands and thousands of online business networking communities.

Remember, not only are you connecting with new business professionals, you are getting potential exposure to their extended networks, which, in the online world, can be infinite. Relationships established online can last a lifetime and may even evolve into "in person" meetings. For example, visit www.MeetUp.com. This is a community of like-minded individuals who share a common interest and meet up in their respective communities.

Anne is convinced that if you want to grow your business, both locally and globally, you must learn to leverage these online business networking resources.

INNER CIRCLE

Are you looking to increase your network? Obviously by reading this book, you are learning about me and my business philosophy. Whether you realize it or not, I have become part of your network (someone that you have come to know). If you have read this far in the book, then you are serious about creating your own destiny. I want to help you achieve this goal.

As a result of being in your network, I would fully expect you to leverage me, my passions, my skills, and my network. If you agree with me, I think you will enjoy learning more about our Inner Circle club. I have a private Inner Circle Publishing Club only for clients who have hired me to coach them in publishing, book promotion, and speaking. More importantly, I also have a public Inner Circle that anyone can join—including you.

Let me ask you a few questions to see if you may be interested. Are you unhappy at work? Is your business struggling? Are you tired of the financial chaos in your life? Do you want an accountability partner in your life? Do you want more *time*, more *money*, more *freedom*, more *health*, more *love*, and more *happiness* in your life?

If you answered "yes" to any of these questions, I invite you right now to leverage me and my network by joining my Inner Circle. My Inner Circle is a group of people who dial into my inspirational calls at the beginning of each week to hear me deliver a live inspirational message directly to club members. The purpose of the call is to help give you that extra bit of adrenaline you may need to help you do your best that week as you pursue your goals and your destiny.

Each call is one-hour long and includes a 45-minute presentation and 15 minutes of question and answer time. You and other club members can ask anything you want. My goal is to provide you with inspiration, energy, resources, techniques, ideas, and strategies to help you dream, plan, execute, and soar in life.

What does it cost? Each weekly call costs about the same as a cup of coffee. All calls are recorded and can be accessed 24/7 via my web site in case you miss the call. When you join, you will also get some really cool free stuff directly from me.

For more information on the Inner Circle club, and to join today, visit my web site at www.CreateYourOwnDestiny.com and click on "Inner Circle." I look forward to serving as your personal accountability partner and to help you realize your destiny!

SUMMARY

My challenge to you is to take the major leadership role in your life and in your business. No one else will do it for you!

One of the greatest lessons I have learned is how powerful your friendships can be. I have had many failures and many successes in life. Through it all, I have developed and nurtured more and more friendships throughout the world on this journey called "life."

As I meet more people, I naturally want to help lead them to success. Therefore, I leverage my network in any way I can to help my friends achieve their goals. In return they do the same for me. Leveraging is not something we should be ashamed of or afraid to do. Remember, as an employee, the whole system is leveraging you and you are getting nothing more than a paycheck. As a business owner, you are leveraging many, and the result is that you will help many more people in the process. Remember to leverage your network, as that is exactly what the extremely wealthy do on a regular basis.

If you don't believe me, ask yourself where Ford Motor Company would be today had it not been for Ford leveraging the knowledge of Firestone? Next, remember that regardless of how good you are at selling, it is important to partner with others via joint venture partnerships and tap into their networks. In doing so, pay your joint venture partners well for their efforts.

I challenge you to look for mentors and to be a mentor. If you are not where you want to be financially, keep an open mind and evaluate the Destiny Achievers Club. If you are struggling in your business, look for business coaches who have "been there and done that."

Most important, leverage the Internet. Explode your business on a global scale and develop friends all over the world. Finally, if you are looking for an accountability partner, consider joining the Inner Circle.

When you build a large network of friends all over the world, make sure you leverage this network. In doing so, I promise you that you will experience more *money*, more *freedom*, and more *love* in life. The kind of love I am talking about is the kind of love and support that only a friend can offer.

CHAPTER 14

Developing Your Higher Calling

When you were born, you cried and the world rejoiced!
Live your life in a manner in which, when you die,
the world cries and you rejoice.
—Indian Proverb

B y now you should be well on the way to living your destiny: you know what you want out of life, you're taking action on a daily basis, and you're prepared to overcome obstacles, risks, and adversities that lie in your way.

You will become a success; I'm certain of it. In fact, Henry David Thoreau said:

"If one advances confidently in the direction of his dreams, and endeavors to live the life in which he has imagined, he will meet with a success unexpected in common hours."[1]

Success will happen. When it comes, what are you going to do? Are you going to keep all your success to yourself? Or are you going to give of your time, your energy, and your money? When you do become a success, I'd like to press upon you a final thought: develop your higher calling.

WHAT IS A HIGHER CALLING?

A higher calling is something that you do above and beyond your destiny; in other words, it's the something that you do to give back to the world.

For many, this might be faith. For others, it might be family or some other worthwhile cause. This higher calling is different for everyone. I challenge you to seek out and develop yours.

As Mother Teresa said:

"I do not pray for success, I ask for faithfulness."[2]

Mother Teresa, possibly more than anyone, devoted almost her entire life to living out her higher calling by founding a mission in Calcutta, India, and devoting her life to helping the poor. When she died on September 5, 1997, I am sure she rejoiced at a time when the world cried!

Many professional athletes today come from modest backgrounds. Once they make it to the big leagues, they have the resources to give a tremendous amount of money back to their communities.

Take Alex Rodriquez, for example. He's a professional baseball player who played for the Seattle Mariners for seven years. I watched him come up through the ranks to become the premier shortstop in Major League Baseball. In the early 1990s, he was a high school student. After the 2000 season, he signed a new contract with the Texas Rangers for $252 million (before becoming a New York Yankee). That's right—more than a quarter of a billion dollars. That's a lot of money by anyone's count. With a higher calling combined with his looks, personality, charisma, and money, Alex Rodriquez can help impact the world for the better.

Alex has chosen to give millions of dollars of his money and countless hours of his time to the kids of inner-city Miami in an effort to help them overcome many of the adversities they face every day.

I know what you're probably thinking: it's easy to give money away and make a difference if you're a multi-millionaire. That may be easy, but I also believe anyone can make a difference in the world regardless of how much you have to give. How? By giving of your time and energy.

Whether you realize it or not, we are all capable of changing the world if each of us were to reach out within our own communities and help feed, clothe, and nourish those in need. One person at a time, each of us can make a difference.

Read this poem by Randy Poole to see how you can make a difference regardless of your age or level of income. This poem will give you a whole new perspective on life. It will make you realize just how much of an impact one individual can have by reaching out and helping those in need.

THE DIFFERENCE HE MADE

Amidst the morning mist of the swift returning tide

I set out on my daily run, my Walkman on my side.

Lost within my private world apart from cares and woes

I ran along the moistened shore, the sand between my toes.

In the distance, I saw a boy, as busy as can be.

He was running, stooping, picking up, and tossing in the sea.

Just what he threw, I couldn't tell, I looked as I drew near.

It seemed to be a rock or shell—as I approached him I could hear.

'Back you go, where you belong. You're safe now hurry home.

Your family's waiting for you little starfish, hurry on!'

It seemed the evening tide had washed the starfish on the shore,

And the swift receding water left a thousand there or more.

And this self-appointed savior, was trying one-by-one

To toss them back into the sea, against the racing sun.

I saw his plight was hopeless, that most of them would die.

I called out from my private world, 'Hey Kid, why even try?'

'Must be at least a thousand here, strewn along the beach,

And even if you had the time, most you'll never reach.

You really think it makes a difference, to waste your time this way?'

And then I paused and waited, just to hear what he would say.

He stooped and took another, and looked me in the eye.

'It makes a difference to this one sir, this starfish will not die!'

With that, he tossed the little life, back where there was hope.

He stooped to take another. I could tell this was no joke.

The words that he spoke to me cut like a surgeon's knife.

Where I saw only numbers, he saw only life.

He didn't see the multitude of starfish on the sand.

He only saw the little life he held there in his hand.

He didn't stop to argue, to prove that he was right.

He just kept tossing starfish in the sea with all his might.

So I too stooped, and picked up, and I tossed into the sea,

And I thought, just what a difference that this boy has made
in me.[3]

Consider what you can learn from the boy in the starfish
poem, and ways you can help improve your family, your community, and the world:

- Spending more time at home with your family.
- Volunteering for neighborhood or community boards or
  committees.

- Ending domestic and sexual violence.

- Becoming involved in a worldwide cause.

- Coaching a kids' sports team.

- Donating food to food banks.

- Rescuing animals.

- Donating money or clothes to worthy organizations.

- Volunteering your time in a church group.

- Even just saving a sea creature that has been washed ashore.

EXERCISE

Reflect for a moment, then list all the many ways you can make a difference in the world.

_____

_____

_____

_____

_____

_____

_____

_____

_____

_____

The opportunities to make a difference are numerous. What's more, they're all around you. Seek them out, then devote your time, energy, passion, and—if you can—your money. I am currently developing my higher calling. You may not know what your higher calling is yet—but thinking about a higher calling is a good start. I have two boys, and through them I have learned how much I enjoy children. It disturbs me to learn that, according to UNICEF, each year 6,000,000 children around the world die because of malnutrition.

My higher calling is guided by my faith and is dedicated to help the children of the world who are in need. I help influence the youth of today to become the leaders of tomorrow.

Truett Cathy, founder of Chick-fil-A and foster parent to more than 120 children, has inspired my higher calling, which is to own and operate foster homes for children in need. I want to help these children avoid addictions of drugs and alcohol and help them become the leaders of tomorrow.

EXERCISE

What is your higher calling in life?

_____

_____

_____

_____

_____

_____

_____

_____

DEFINITION OF SUCCESS

We've talked a great deal in this chapter about success and your higher calling. Those are great, worthy topics. But I'd like you to consider this thought: achieving your destiny and obtaining success are never endpoints; never something you can obtain and then never find again. Ben Sweetland said:

"Success is a journey, not a destination."[4]

To make your journey in life a fulfilling one, consider this definition of success by Ralph Waldo Emerson:

"To laugh often and much; to win the respect of intelligent people, and the affection of children; to earn the appreciation of honest critics and endure the betrayal of false friends; to appreciate beauty; to find the best in others; to leave the world a little better, whether by a healthy child, a garden patch, or a redeemed social condition; to know even one life has breathed easier because you have lived. This is the meaning of success."[5]

Castaway, starring Tom Hanks, is one of my favorite movies as it symbolizes the essence of choice better than any other movie I have ever seen. While everyone was caught up in the plane crash and his living on a deserted island for so long, I was impacted the most at the end of the movie after he delivered the last FedEx package. At this point, while very far out in the middle of nowhere, he came to a crossroad. He looked in each direction as far as the eye could see. In doing so, for maybe the first time in his life, he was able to choose which road to travel. For probably the first time, he used his heart as his compass to choose which direction to travel. I challenge you to do the same. I believe that if you listen to your heart and then choose your own destiny, you will pursue a higher calling at the same time. Which direction do you choose to go? This is your choice regardless of the other influences in your life.

This scene at the end of the movie reminds me of what J. Martin Kohe once said:

"The greatest power that a person possesses is the
power to choose"[6]

SUMMARY

Now that you have almost completed this book, you, too, may
be at a crossroads. I challenge you to travel down the road your
heart desires. But remember, whichever road you choose, please go
in a manner so our world will be a better place because of you and
what you have given back.

Here's another quote by T. Menlo that I believe best illus-
trates the concept of developing a higher calling:

"If each day of your life represents a sparkle of light,
at your life's end you will have illuminated the world."[7]

To each of you reading this book, you individually (not
anyone else) will sooner or later need to determine what your
higher calling is in life. It is different for each of us, but I hope that
you identify it—and that you devote your life to helping others in a
way no one else can.

As you develop your higher calling and give back to the world
and to those in need, you will ultimately become a more fulfilled
individual and also experience more *love* and more *happiness* as a
result of your efforts.

I challenge you to seek out your higher calling and then
illuminate the world on your journey. You are doing great things
and you are about to do even greater things. Enjoy life and live
every day by treating it like the precious gift that it really is. I would
like to end this chapter with a quote from Charles Dickens:

"No one is useless in this world who lightens the
burden of it for anyone else."[8]

CHAPTER **15**

Leaving Your Legacy

The great use of life is to spend it for
something that will outlast it.
—William James[1]

As a professional speaker, I constantly meet people in my
audiences who tell me that they have achieved virtually all
of their goals in life but are still unhappy. It doesn't seem to make
any sense.

Perhaps you aren't as happy as you'd like to be. My theory is
that we have all been brainwashed into believing that the American
dream means having the nicest cars, houses, clothes, and other toys.
But I believe that the things we seek out don't make us happy. After
the initial joy of purchasing these items wears off, we still feel
unfulfilled.

My father once told me,

"The more possessions you have, the less freedom you have."

At the time, I was 15 or 16, so of course I didn't believe him.
However, 20 years later, I have come to see and believe the truth in
what he said.

Why is it that so many people today are so unhappy in a time
of prosperity never experienced by any other generation? I
believe it's because we have been programmed to work for the
wrong reasons. When is the right time to stop pursuing money
and start pursuing freedom, joy, happiness, and fulfillment? You
are the only one who can answer this question. Why do so many

people fail to find happiness even though they pursued wealth their whole lives? They may have also missed out on love, fulfillment, and peace of mind.

GREED AND MATERIALISM

I think many people never find fulfillment because they are pursuing the wrong things. They are pursuing money instead of happiness. Ask yourself this question: how much money is enough? Let me explain further.

According to much of our popular entertainment and advertising, people find happiness and fulfillment only when they live in enormous houses, drive sports cars, wear expensive clothes, and dine in chic restaurants. It's my belief that we are programmed to believe this from the moment we first watch television. Yes, it takes money to live. However, I believe that money is not more important than:

- Family

- Friendships

- Children

- Animals (pets)

- Health

- Wellness

- Peace of mind

- Happiness

Often we get our priorities mixed up and our families, friendships, children, and health all suffer as a result. Consider this proverb:

"Money is a good servant but a bad master."

Despite what we see in TV and in the movies, life is *not* a race to see who can acquire the most toys and the most wealth. This kind of race is not really winnable. There will always be *someone* with more time, more toys, and more wealth than what you and I have. More important, the race to wealth is beside the point—if your wealth comes at the cost of your well-being and you find yourself unhappy, you haven't really won much of anything.

I believe that instead of pursuing your dream home, your dream car, and other dream possessions, you should pursue your dream *life*.

HAPPINESS

Too many people find themselves unhappy, despite material abundance, because they are following someone else's idea of what their destinies should be instead of creating their own. Many people find that they're working, not because they enjoy their work, but because they need a paycheck. Ask yourself this question: are you working out of need, or out of choice?

Many people work primarily out of need. As a result, their level of happiness is diminished. Often we look to other people to make us happy when we are not finding happiness within our careers. I think one of the reasons divorce is so rampant is that people often look to their spouses to make them happy. Spouses may be able to make their partners feel happy for a while, but eventually it doesn't work. We must not look to others to find our joy and happiness; instead, we must create happiness within ourselves. I like how author Dr. Melba Colgrove put it when she said:

"Joy is the feeling of grinning on the inside."[2]

You must make your own happiness. No one and no thing is capable of making you happy, as happiness is a gift that you choose to give yourself each day. No one can take it from you, regardless of the many adversities you may face.

I can't emphasize this enough—other people cannot make you happy. I think poet James Oppenheim hit the nail on the head when he said:

"The foolish man seeks happiness in the distance;
　　the wise man grows it under his feet."[3]

When we look to ourselves for happiness while pursuing our passions, we will find happiness and leave a legacy for others to benefit from or be inspired by as a result.

Happiness is doing what you love, pursuing your passions, helping other people along the way, living for a cause, freely loving others, and achieving financial and emotional peace of mind.

As you become happier, I believe that you will become unstoppable and live a life like you have never envisioned. You will create your own destiny and leave a legacy for others to benefit from forever. As the famous mathematician Archimedes said:

"Give me a lever long enough and a fulcrum on which
　　to place it and I shall move the world."[4]

Make this your new mantra, and your daily actions will, over time, literally change the world.

YOUR GIFT TO THE WORLD

We are all faced with the challenge to find a cause, a mission, a belief, or something that we could do, day and night, to make the world a better place. Your challenge is to build a legacy, to live by theologian John Wesley's credo:

"Do all the good you can,
By all the means you can,
In all the ways you can,
In all the places you can,

> At all times you can,
> To all people you can,
> As long as ever you can."[5]

This is a big challenge. But we must learn to live by this creed. If you are looking for ways to volunteer your time and serve others in your community or throughout the world, I encourage you to join your local Rotary Club so that you can make a difference. I particularly like Rotary International's mission of "service above self," and I encourage you to learn more about this humanitarian organization at www.Rotary.org.

Whether through Rotary International or many of the other great organizations out there serving others, I challenge you to share your expertise. Share your passions, your skills. Become a coach or a mentor. Help make your community a better place. If you are having a hard time finding exciting ways to improve your community, visit www.HelpYourCommunity.org.

You can give your money, your time, or your expertise. Give to your local youth. Give freely with no expectation of return. Teach others to give of themselves. Consider this an opportunity to pursue your lifelong passions.

EXERCISE

What are your gifts? What mission can you get behind to make the world a better place? What do you want your legacy to be?

_____

_____

_____

_____

_____

_____

SOARING

Have you ever felt discontented, lonely, perhaps that your life was unfulfilled? Have you ever achieved a goal, yet still remained unhappy? Have you ever desired to soar like an eagle?

Perhaps you have a soaring spirit inside of you waiting to be unleashed. Perhaps you have passions yet to be discovered, pursued, or enjoyed. If you have ever felt this way, then you will understand what Helen Keller meant when she said:

"One can never consent to creep when one feels
an impulse to soar."[6]

Now is the time to take action and soar in life. I challenge you to make permanent changes, pursue your passions, create your own happiness, and leave a lasting legacy.

Consider the amazing story of Cliff Young. Cliff lived an average life as a potato farmer in Australia, mostly keeping to himself until, at age 57, he began pursuing a new passion for long-distance running. Soon he was often seen in the countryside training in a raincoat and gumboots, as he lived in a very wet region.

After a few years of training, he shocked the world when, at age 61, he won the first Sydney-to-Melbourne ultra-marathon—a distance of 875 kilometers (nearly 545 miles). To run this distance at any age is quite a feat, but to run it at 61 and beat some of the best-conditioned athletes in the world, some of whom were a third his age, is absolutely incredible.

For years, experts in the sport of running believed that the body needed a certain amount of sleep per night when running almost 100 miles a day. However, after falling way behind on the first day, Cliff awoke at 1:00 AM and ran throughout the night. He surpassed the leaders, who slept through till 5:00 AM. His strategy worked so well that he continued to wake and start running four hours earlier than his competitors. As a result, he astonished the world when he crossed the finish line in first place after 5 days, 15 hours, and 4 minutes.

The news of Cliff Young's shocking victory quickly traveled throughout Australia, since no one thought he'd have a chance—especially since he was facing the country's best long-distance runners. He became a legend, and the nation fell in love with this 61-year-old potato farmer who saw the invisible and achieved the impossible.

He finished the same race again in 1984 and in 1987 at ages 62 and 65, and now his strategy of waking at 1:00 AM instead of 5:00 AM is widely practiced in this event. He broke a paradigm, overcame self-doubt, and accomplished what no one in the world thought he could. He left a legacy of innovation and inspiration by pursuing his passions and not following the limiting beliefs held by so many others.

Now consider the true story of another legend who attained happiness and left a legacy. At the age of 66 (after most of his life had passed), Harlan Sanders decided he wanted to go into the fried chicken business. He had what he absolutely believed to be the best fried chicken recipe in the world.

He started out by going to restaurants in his community and offering the owners his recipe if they would give him a small percentage of their increase in fried chicken sales. No one was interested, so he traveled in his old car, pitching his recipe from town to town all across the country. He was rejected time and time again. At times, due to little or no cash flow, he even slept in his car.

He did this for two years and was turned down over 2,000 times. He never gave up, and soon thereafter, someone did buy his recipe and it caught on. He certainly lived by the "next" mentality that I believe is a requirement for all entrepreneurs. Harlan Sanders became the multimillionaire "Colonel Sanders" of Kentucky Fried Chicken before he passed on at 96 years old.

Age, health, and other circumstances should not hold you back from pursing your passions, making a difference in this world, and leaving a legacy for others. No doubt about it, Cliff Young and Colonel Sanders soared in life, and you can do the same.

EXERCISE

What legacy would you leave for your family, community, or the world if you pursued your true passions?

_____

_____

_____

_____

_____

_____

_____

_____

_____

SUMMARY

Leaving a legacy is not easy but I believe it is certainly worth pursuing. Think of the hardships and adversities Cliff Young overcame after running nonstop for almost six days before crossing the finish line to victory. Think of all those cold nights that Colonel Sanders slept in his car, contemplating giving up. As author Richard Bach wrote:

"Dream what you dare to dream. Be where you want to go.
Be what you want to be. Live."[7]

I hope that this chapter will encourage you to seek happiness within yourself and not through materialism. I challenge you to give back to the world, help others in need, and share your wisdom, experience, and knowledge for the benefit of mankind.

If you do these things, I promise that you will indeed *soar*, leave your legacy, and achieve more *happiness* in life.

CHAPTER 16

Asking Yourself the Ultimate Destiny Questions

For what shall it profit a man, if he shall gain
the whole world, and lose his own soul?
—Mark 8:36

This book is not a book on theology. In fact, I struggled with whether or not to include this section in my book. All of the so-called experts advised me not to bring up the issue of God for fear that it could turn away some readers.

I am not a minister, nor am I even qualified to write about faith and the belief in God (or lack thereof). As a result, you will see little mention of this topic anywhere else in this book.

However, in thinking over this issue, I finally decided that I would be doing my readers a disservice to write a book about destiny and not pose the following questions. I decided to include this section in my book and will share with you my beliefs on faith, since so many readers have asked about what I believe.

LIFE'S BIGGEST QUESTIONS

What is your ultimate destiny? What happens to you after your time on earth is through? Do you believe in God? Do you believe in life after death?

I want to challenge you. My challenge is for you to determine your beliefs about your creator and your ultimate destiny. Without God, I believe that much of life does not make sense and your search for greater meaning in life will never end. For example, many people search for fulfillment in the wrong places with the zealous pursuit of money and through material consumption.

But with God, I believe that true fulfillment in life is attainable. I also believe that God decides our ultimate destiny in life. However, it doesn't really matter what I believe. What is important here is for you to determine what your beliefs are, what has shaped and influenced your beliefs over time, and why you feel the way you do. One of my quotes I termed many years ago says:

"Only those who can see the invisible can
achieve the impossible."

For many people, God is invisible. But for those who can see God's presence in their life, their faith and belief will bring them fulfillment and allow them to do great things while making a huge contribution to this world. If you have a belief in God and in your own vision, you will become unstoppable in life and repeatedly create a greater good for humanity. I believe that with God, all things are possible.

However, some people argue that it is not honorable to strive for great achievements on earth if you want to shape your ultimate destiny in God's eye. My view on this issue is that it is important to strive for both. Live your life in a way so that you work hard to attain your goals, but while doing so, continuously look for ways to give back and help others in need. Chapter 14 of this book was designed to address this challenge.

In case you are wondering how I arrived at this point in my life with regards to my faith, let me share with you how I became the person I am today. When I was 17 years old, as you may recall, my goal was to play in the NFL. The summer before graduating from high school, I attended a Fellowship of Christian Athletes sports camp, where I selected football as my sport of emphasis. During this week, in addition to football, I was exposed to Jesus Christ (in a way that I had never been before). As a result, I realized that, even if I achieved my goal of making it to the pros and perhaps even winning a Super Bowl ring, the exhilaration of winning a championship on earth would only be temporary.

However, by following Christ, I realized that a championship with God in heaven would last an eternity. As a result of this revelation, I accepted Jesus Christ in my heart as my personal Lord and Savior during the summer of 1986. Since then, He has been my co-pilot and has steered me toward my true destiny in life of helping others succeed. I believe that my life is a gift from God and that my gift back to God is what I make of my life.

I hope that by writing *Creating Your Own Destiny*, I have helped you on your journey in life and that you ponder this message on faith as my gift to you. I am not trying to tell you what to believe, I am just telling you what I believe and how following Christ has positively impacted my life.

TWENTY-FIRST CENTURY DILEMMA

I am challenging you, perhaps for the first time, to take a leading role in your life and actually create your own destiny. You may be reluctant to do this, believing that it is arrogant or contradictory to God's divine design for your life to pursue your own passions and career goals. I would argue that in doing so, you are actually living by our Creator's plan, because we were built to use our free will.

The U.S. Constitution was conceived by people who believed we were created by God and entrusted with free will to shape our destinies—life, liberty, and the pursuit of happiness. Whether you are an American or not, these can be shared values. My belief is that you reap what you sow and it all must be done in harmony with God's love.

God gives us the freedom to choose our destinies and the free will to act (or not) on our passions. God gives us the strength to overcome all adversities, all obstacles, and all rejections. God gives us the determination to never give up on pursuing our goals—no matter how much the odds are stacked against us. God gives us the ability to experience the miracles that somehow find their way in our lives as a result of the blood, sweat, and tears we shed pursuing our destinies.

We achieve ultimate joy in life when we align our free will with our goals, mission, and higher calling with God's divine destiny and direction in our lives. When in doubt, and when facing adversity, ask for God's assistance, spirit, and strength and you will ultimately create your own destiny and soar in life!

The real win as a result of creating your own destiny is that your gift and successes contribute to the world and can be an example for others to follow, which ultimately leaves a legacy from which others can benefit.

This journey is not going to be easy. Your faith in God will be tested, challenged, and certainly put to use as you stay true to your core convictions and live a life that makes God proud to be your Creator. Through your challenging times, what can be the ultimate resource that guides you through life's storms?

THE ANSWER

If this chapter has inspired you to think about these questions, then I believe that the answers you seek can be found through reading the Bible and applying its principles in your daily life. Many of life's most compelling issues can be resolved by applying the wisdom offered in this amazing book that is as relevant today as it was thousands of years ago. If you are to truly create your own destiny, then I challenge you to pick up a Bible and not just read it, but study it on a regular basis and you will find how the words will help you in both times of calm and crisis. In doing so, I know you will benefit greatly. All the world's traditions and cultures use sacred texts as their guides. Mine is the Bible. What is yours?

EXERCISE

What are your beliefs about God?

_____

_____

_____

_____

_____

What are your beliefs about life after death?

_____

_____

_____

_____

_____

What events in your life have shaped your beliefs on this subject?

_____

_____

_____

_____

_____

What is your ultimate destiny?

_____

_____

_____

_____

_____

_____

SUMMARY

The philosophy I have covered in this chapter is a universal and enduring truth we can all live by. As we launch our creative destinies, we model for others (including our children) that they can, too!

With God in your heart, I believe you can help shape your ultimate destiny in life. I challenge you to seek out your faith so that you can have God at your side as you travel along your journey in pursuit of your goals—both in your life, on earth, and beyond.

Achieving Your Destiny

Thoughts lead on to purposes,
purposes go forth in action,
action forms habits,
habits decide character,
and character fixes our destiny.
—Tryon Edwards[1]

Well, this is my story. I hope that in some way you have been inspired and have benefited from my thoughts and suggestions. After reading this book, I hope that you will believe what William Jennings Bryan once said:

"Destiny is not a matter of chance, it is a matter of choice.
It is not a thing to be waited for, it is a thing to be achieved."[2]

As I close, I want you to understand that life is full of choices and that you must take charge of your life by choosing your destiny and moving forward with confidence and determination. Always remember what Yogi Berra said:

"If you don't know where you are going,
any road will take you there."[3]

I hope the material in this book has inspired you to further discover the destiny for which you were born. If not, I challenge you to consistently go through my Success Road Map to help guide your way through this challenging world in which we all live.

Success Road Map

1. Visualize your dreams.

2. Set big goals.

3. Put your family ahead of work.

4. Build real wealth.

5. Create your game plan.

6. Conquer adversity, temptation, and addiction.

7. Overcome your fears.

8. Remember those who molded you.

9. Execute your plan daily.

10. Grow your business on a limited budget.

11. Choose health, nutrition, and exercise daily.

12. Make permanent changes in your life.

13. Lead and leverage your network.

14. Develop your higher calling.

15. Leave your legacy.

16. Ask yourself the ultimate destiny questions.

The point of this whole soul-searching process—and this book specifically—is that the gift we are all born with is the free choice to take control of our lives; to choose our own destinies. The only way to take control of our lives is through our goals.

We can take control of our lives and destiny . . . *simply by writing out our future in advance!* By doing so, we can create our own destinies. It was Peter Drucker who said:

"The best way to predict the future is to create it."[4]

I urge you to get started immediately by taking advantage of the freedom that we all enjoy and decide once and for all:

Exactly what it is in life that you want!

Once you have finally discovered your destiny, I challenge you to plow forward and develop the courage to pursue it by taking action and executing your game plan on a daily basis.

I wrote this book to act as your road map and compass; to help direct and guide you as you pursue your life goals. I challenge you to incorporate the ideas, techniques, and strategies summarized in this book, so that you will ultimately experience what most people want—more *time*, more *money*, more *freedom*, more *health*, more *love*, and more *happiness*.

Some people spend their whole lives *preparing* to live, but they never *live*. Even though much of this book is about planning your *future*, I still think it is extremely important to enjoy the present moment and live *today*. Henry Van Dyke said in his poem, *Seize the Day*:

"Be glad of life, because it gives you the chance to love and to work and to play and to look up at the stars."[5]

If you execute your plan daily and pursue your goals and destiny, make absolutely certain that you want what you are pursuing. Dale Carnegie said it best:

"Success is getting what you want, happiness is wanting what you get."[6]

Now that you have completed this book, I am hopeful that you are ready to fully comprehend the *Destiny Secret* that I alluded to in the Introduction. This secret has become my personal philosophy. It is something I have developed after 20 years of intense study in the field of personal growth and development.

This secret, if adopted into your life, will be all the knowledge that you need to experience what the subtitle of this book promises:

"How to Get Exactly What You Want Out of Life and Work."

At 2:30 AM on the morning of March 16, 2002, I had a revelation, and I woke up out of a deep sleep to write my *Destiny Secret* (see page 232).

If you take nothing more away from my book, always remember two things: My *Destiny Secret* and what author, Nobel and Pulitzer Prize winner Pearl S. Buck said:

> "The young do not know enough to be prudent,
> and therefore they attempt the impossible—
> and achieve it generation after generation."[7]

Whether you are young or old, if your belief in your vision is strong enough, you can accomplish the impossible time and time again. You are a living magnet and you attract what you envision. Whatever you want, wants you!

Nowhere in this book did I say that creating your own destiny would be easy or without your share of pain. In fact, achieving one's destiny may be one of the most difficult challenges that we ultimately face in life. However, I am a firm believer in what seven-time Tour de France champion and cancer survivor Lance Armstrong said in his book, *Every Second Counts*, about pursuing one's dreams:

> "Be brave and fight like hell!
> Pain is temporary but quitting lasts forever."[8]

I encourage you to never give up on pursuing your destiny and fight as if your life depended on it—because it does! Ultimately, I believe that your level of happiness in life is partly dependent on whether or not you stay true to your dreams. Always remember that it is not over until you win. Winning takes commitment and determination. Poet Henry Wadsworth Longfellow said:

"The heights by great men achieved and kept,
were not attained by a sudden fight,
but while their companions slept,
kept toiling upward in the night."[9]

Creating your own destiny is a lifelong battle within your mind where you take action every day to fulfill your dreams. It is a battle that you will win when you set your intention and continue on with persistence. Finally, remember William Shakespeare's quote:

"It is not in the stars to hold our destiny,
but in ourselves."[10]

Now that I have shared my philosophy, I hope that you will contact me to share your dreams and goals. Perhaps I can help you achieve them. As you move on from here pursuing your destiny, my final challenge to you is this: live your life as Mother Teresa lived hers. I challenge you to live your life in a manner in which, when you die, the world cries and you rejoice.

This process will be a long journey. I encourage you to take the time to kick back and enjoy the beaches of your life. May your life be filled with peace, love, prosperity, and the achievement of your destiny!

Thank you and God bless. I appreciate you.

Your friend,

Patrick Snow

Destiny Secret

"Once you decide what you really want out of life and work, your mind will be your only obstacle and your only competition!

When you start to believe and trust in yourself and in your own unique passions, you will conquer your mind's self-limiting beliefs. These limiting beliefs are the only roadblock or obstacle that can hold you back from getting all of what you really want.

Once you have made the decision to overcome your fears, conquer all of your self-doubt, and win the battle of your mind, you will accomplish everything you have ever envisioned.

Your mind will have ignited a fire in your heart to execute your plan by taking daily actions in pursuit of your goals. As you experience this, you will become an unstoppable force of power, fully capable of achieving more success and freedom than you could have ever imagined.

Once you have done this, you will literally Create Your Own Destiny!"

—Patrick Snow
www.CreateYourOwnDestiny.com
(800) 951-7721

NOTES

INTRODUCTION

1. Wallace, Randall, screenwriter for *Braveheart* (film). 2005. Icon Entertainment International.
2. Ringer, Robert. *Million Dollar Habits* (New York: Ballantine Books, 1991), 51.
3. Nightingale, Earl. *Lead the Field* (Nices, IL: Nightingale-Conant, 2002).
4. Eliot, T. S. *On Poetry and Poets* (New York: Farrar, Straus, and Cudahy, 1957), 360.
5. Emerson, Ralph W. *Essays and Lectures* (New York: Library of America, 1983).
6. Buck, Pearl S. *The Goddess Abides* (New York: Pocket, 1972).
7. Ceasar, Julius. www.FamousQuotes.com.
8. Holmes, Oliver Wendell. *The Autocrat of the Breakfast Table* (Boston, MA: Houghton, Mifflin, and Co., 1893).

CHAPTER 1

1. Wright, Frank Lloyd. Architect. (1869–1959)
2. Stone, W. Clement. www.FamousQuotes.com.
3. St. Augustine, Roman Church Father. *Sermons*, 43, 1.
4. Morrison, Alex. www.FamousQuotes.com.
5. Bryant, Paul "Bear." In J. Dent. *The Junction Boys* (New York: St. Martin's Griffin, 2000).
6. Robbins, Anthony. *Awaken the Giant Within* (New York: Simon & Schuster, 1992).
7. Robino, Toni Ann. *Inspiring Breakthrough Secrets to Live Your Dreams* (Lake Placid, NY: Aviva, 2002), 22.
8. Olsen, Larry. *Get a Vision and Live It.* (Harrison, NY: Book Clearing House, 2008).
9. Hillel. *Pirke: Avot*, 1:14.

CHAPTER 2

1. Prochnow, Herbert. *Toastmaster's Handbook* (Upper Saddle River, NJ: Prentice Hall, 1949).

2. Kennedy, John F. Raleigh, NC, September 17, 1960.
3. Anthony, Robert. *Beyond Positive Thinking: A No-Nonsense Formula for Getting the Results You Want* (Newport News, VA: Morgan James, 2004), 66.
4. Hunt, W. L. www.FamousQuotes.com.
5. Nightingale, Earl. *The Strangest Secret*, 1956.

CHAPTER 3

1. Witcraft, Forest. "Within My Power." *Scouting*, October 1950.
2. *USA Today*, August 22, 2002.
3. Stanley, Thomas, and William Danko. *The Millionaire Next Door* (New York: Simon & Schuster, 1996).
4. Confucius. www.FamousQuotes.com.
5. Atkinson, John. www.FamousQuotes.com.
6. Hill, Napoleon. www.FamousQuotes.com.
7. Nietzsche, Fredrick. *Twilight of the Idols*. Germany, 1889.
8. Ford, Henry. *My Life and Work* (Garden City, NY: Garden City Publishing, 1922).
9. Edison, Thomas A. In Hedstrom, D. From *Telegraph to Light Bulb with Thomas Edison* (Nashville, TN: B&H Publishing Group, 2007), 22.
10. Goldstein, Sam, and Robert B. Brooks. *Handbook of Resilience in Children* (New York: Springer, 2006), 305.

CHAPTER 4

1. Carnegie, Andrew. "The Best Fields for Philanthropy," *North American Review*, December 1889, 684.
2. *ABC News*, December 5, 2008.
3. *USA Today*, August 22, 2002.
4. *USA Today*, December 5, 2002.
5. "The High Cost of Disengaged Employees." *Gallup Management Journal*, 2002.
6. CNN, 2002.
7. The Sloan Work and Family Research Center, Boston: Boston College.
8. Socrates. In Xenophen. *Conversations of Socrates*. (New York, Penguin Classics, 1990).
9. Chew, Danny, phone interview with author.

CHAPTER 5

1. Allen, James. *As a Man Thinketh* (The Floating Press, 1902).
2. Stein, Ben. *How Successful People Win: Using Bunkhouse Logic to Get What You Want in Life* (New York: Hay House, 2005), 17.
3. Cocteau, Jean. *Cocteau's World: An Anthology of Writings* (New York: Dodd Mead, 1972), 305.
4. Greenwald, Crawford. www.FamousQuotes.com.
5. Montaigne, Michel de. *The Complete Essays of Montaigne* (Stanford, CA: Stanford University Press, 1958).

CHAPTER 6

1. *Without Limits* (film), 1998.
2. Norris, David. www.FamousQuotes.com.
3. *Two Wolves*. www.firstpeople.us/FP-Html-Legends/TwoWolves-Cherokee.html.
4. Epictetus. *Discourses and Selected Writings* (New York: Penguin Classics, 2008).
5. Roosevelt, Franklin Delano. *Kansas City Start*, June 5, 1977.
6. Dyer, Ron, personal interview with author on Dyer's philosophy.
7. Eardley, Stephen. *Blessings*. "Reconnections & New Directions," 2003 Conference, Lester B. Pearson College.

CHAPTER 7

1. Hale, Sarah J. *A Dictionary of Thoughts*, 1907.
2. Schwartz, David Joseph. *The Magic of Thinking Big* (New York: Fireside, 1987), 234.
3. www.FamousQuotes.com.
4. www.FamousQuotes.com.
5. Pontiere, S. EzineArticles.com, June 2008.
6. www.FamousQuotes.com.
7. Friedman, Susan A. *Inspiring Breakthrough Secrets to Live Your Dreams* (Lake Placid, NY: Aviva, 2001), 82.
8. Brown, Les. *Live Your Dreams* (New York: Harper Paperbacks, 1994).
9. Anonymous. Earliest attribution—Columnist Herb Caen (1916–1997), *San Francisco Chronicle*.
10. King Martin Luther, Jr. "I've Been to the Mountain Top." Memphis, Tennessee, April 3, 1968. www.mlkonline.net.

11. Gregory, Dick, as quoted in *Rockford Register Star*, March 2, 2002.
12. France, Anatole. www.FamousQuotes.com.
13. Radmacher, Mary Ann. www.maryanneradmacher.com.
14. Brown, Les. www.FamousQuotes.com.
15. Herbert, Frank. "Bene Gesserit Litany Against Fear," *Dune* (New York: Putnam, 1965).

CHAPTER 8

1. Wilde, Oscar. *The Importance of Being Earnest and Other Plays* (New York: Penguin Classics, 2001), 167.
2. Towne, Charles Hanson. "Around the Corner," *A World of Windows: and other Poems* (New York: George H. Doran, 1919), 66.
3. Lincoln, Abraham. In Baslar, R. (ed.). *The Collected Works of Abraham Lincoln*, Volume II, New Brunswick, NJ, 1953, p. 57.
4. Ziglar, Zig. *Zig Ziglar's Secrets of Closing the Sale* (New York: Berkley, 1984).
5. Gandhi, Mahatma. www.FamousQuotes.com.

CHAPTER 9

1. Addison, John. www.FamousQuotes.com.
2. Franklin, Benjamin. *Poor Richard's Almanack*.
3. Addison, John. *Cato*, 1713, iv, i.
4. Ford, Henry. *Reader's Digest*, 1934.
5. Eliot, T. S. *The Idea of a Christian Society* (New York: Harcourt Brace, 1940).
6. Gide, Andre. www.FamousQuotes.com.
7. Einstein, Albert. www.FamousQuotes.com.
8. McCarrick, Bill, was Patrick Snow's football and baseball coach in grammar school.
9. Twain, Mark. *Mark Twain* (New York: Sheldon & Co., 1871).

CHAPTER 10

1. Tracy, Brian. *The 100 Absolutely Unbreakable Laws of Business Success* (San Francisco: Berrett-Koehler, 2000), 62.
2. Brodine, Brent. www.FamousQuotes.com.
3. Ziglar, Zig. *Zig Ziglar's Secrets of Closing the Sale* (New York: Berkley, 1984).

4. Hall, Doug. *Jump Start Your Business Brain* (Brain Brew Books, 2001).
5. Hilton, Conrad. *Be My Guest* (Englewood Cliffs, NJ: Prentice Hall, 1957).

CHAPTER 11

1. Thoreau, Henry David. *Walden* (New York: E. P. Dutton & Co., 1912), 195.
2. Dewey, John. *Democracy and Education* (New York: Macmillan, 1916), 280.

CHAPTER 12

1. Rohn, Jim. *The Treasury of Quotes* (Irving, TX: Jim Rohn International, 1993).
2. Franklin, Benjamin. *Poor Richard's Almanack*.
3. Robbins, Anthony. *Awaken the Giant Within* (New York: Simon & Schuster, 1992), 249.

CHAPTER 13

1. Hill, Napolean. *Think and Grow Rich* (New York: Ballantine Books, 1960).
2. Darwin, Charles. www.FamousQuotes.com.
3. Mackay Harvey. *The Mackay Performance Scorecard* (web site). www.harveymackay.com/pdfs/scorecard.pdf.
4. Crane, Frank. www.FamousQuotes.com.

CHAPTER 14

1. Thoreau, Henry David. *Walden: or, Life in the Woods*, 1899, p. 340.
2. Mother Teresa. *New York Times*, June 18, 1980.
3. Poole, Randy. "The Difference He Made."
4. Sweetland, Ben. *I Will: A Practical Guide for Utilizing the Powerful Forces of Your Subconcious Mind* (Chatsworth, CA: Wilshire Book Company, 1978).
5. Emerson, Ralph Waldo. www.FamousQuotes.com.
6. Kohe, J. Martin. *Your Greatest Power* (Cleveland: Ralston, 1953).
7. Menlo, T. www.FamousQuotes.com.
8. Dickens, Charles. *Our Mutual Friend*, 1865.

CHAPTER 15

1. James, William. In Compton, C. *William James, Philosopher and Man* (New York: Scarecrow Press, 1957), 191.
2. Colgrove, Melba. www.FamousQuotes.com.
3. Oppenheim, James. *War and Laughter* (New York: Century Co., 1916), 77.
4. Archimedes. 230 BC.
5. Wesley, John. *The Works of the Rev. John Wesley, Volume 10* (New York: J&J Harper, 1827), 271.
6. Keller, Helen. *The Story of My Life* (New York: Doubleday, 1905), 393.
7. Bach, Richard. www.FamousQuotes.com.

A FINAL NOTE

1. Edwards, Tryon. *A Dictionary of Thoughts* (Detroit: F. B. Dickerson, 1908), 114.
2. Bryan, William J. *Speeches of William Jennings Bryan*, Volume 2 (New York: Funk & Wagnalls, 1909).
3. Berra, Yogi. *When You Come to a Fork in the Road, Take It* (New York: Hyperion, 2002).
4. Drucker, Peter. In Edersheim, E. and P. Drucker. *The Definitive Drucker* (New York: McGraw-Hill, 2006), 83.
5. Van Dyke, Henry. *Seize the Day*.
6. Carnegie, Dale. www.dalecarnegie.com.
7. Buck, Pearl S. *The Goddess Abides* (New York: John Day Co., 1972), 80.
8. Armstrong, Lou. *Every Second Counts* (New York: Broadway Books, 2003).
9. Longfellow, Henry W. *The Complete Poetical Works of Longfellow* (Boston: Hughton Mifflin, 1922), 187.
10. Shakespeare, William. *Julius Caesar*, 1599.

ABOUT THE AUTHOR

Patrick Snow is an international best-selling author, professional keynote speaker, publishing coach, and Internet entrepreneur. He firmly believes we can all achieve our individual and organizational destinies when we *"Dream, Plan, Execute, and Soar."* Patrick Snow has electrified and inspired more than 1,500 audiences worldwide over the last 20 years to create their own destinies and get exactly what they want out of life and work. Today, he is known as the "Dean of Destiny" by high achievers nationwide.

After being laid off following 9/11, and again in 2002, from high-tech sales, Patrick retired from corporate America on his own terms at 36 years of age to live the entrepreneurial life he loves. Today, at age 41, he guides and inspires others to turn their career distress into personal success by applying leadership principles, embracing change, balancing family and work, and achieving one's visions!

Patrick discovered his gift for speaking in the fall of 1986 at age 17. As the captain of his high school varsity football team, he delivered the pregame speeches that inspired his team members to perform at their highest levels. He knew at that moment that inspiring others to achieve extraordinary results both at work and at home was his passion in life.

Patrick's "destiny" message has been profiled in the *New York Times*, *Denver Post*, and the *Chicago Sun-Times*. His self-published, best-selling book, *Creating Your Own Destiny: How to Get Exactly What You Want Out of Life and Work*, and his personal transition were also featured as a cover story in *USA TODAY*. Patrick's book has been translated into numerous foreign languages and has sold more than 150,000 copies across six continents since 2001.

Patrick's second book, also being published by Wiley in late 2010, is titled *The Affluent Entrepreneur: 20 Proven Principles for Achieving Prosperity*. Patrick is also a contributing author to numerous other books, including the new *Chicken Soup for the Soul: Life Lessons for Mastering the Law of Attraction*.

To date, Patrick has coached more than 200 clients in achieving their goals of writing, publishing, and marketing their books. He's coached thousands of others to build their businesses and organizations on limited budgets using his "Sales Success Formula" and "Destiny Secret." His warm-hearted style and passion for helping others achieves stunning results in their lives, careers, and businesses that fuels lasting friendships and invites expressions of gratitude from those who follow his time-tested, from-the-trenches, proven system.

Originally from Michigan, Patrick graduated from the University of Montana in 1991. He and his wife of 20 years, Cheryl, are proud parents of two sons, Samuel and Jacob. They reside on Bainbridge Island, Washington.

ABOUT THE SNOW GROUP

After 10 years of speaking, writing, and coaching part-time, Patrick Snow successfully launched The Snow Group as a sole proprietorship at the turn of the millennium on January 1, 2000. Since then, his message has been well received globally, and his book has been translated into numerous languages throughout the world. Patrick Snow has spoken worldwide and has clients on six different continents.

The mission of The Snow Group is to help people worldwide overcome their fears, turn their career distress into personal success, and help others attain more *time*, more *money*, more *freedom*, more *health*, more *love*, and more *happiness* in life. As a business-ownership advocate, Patrick Snow is dedicated to helping others apply his free enterprise philosophy to their lives and achieve wealth and prosperity through capitalism. The Snow Group concentrates its energy in four areas:

Author: This book is available at volume discounts and in numerous
                foreign languages.
Speaker: Patrick will tailor his speech to address your needs.
                www.CreateYourOwnDestiny.com
Coach: www.BestSellerPublishingCoaching.com
                www.BestSellerPublishingInstitute.com
Entrepreneur: www.DestinyAchieversClub.com
                www.OutEarnYourBills.com

For a 30-minute, complimentary consultation or price quote, please visit:

www.PatrickSnow.com

BEST-SELLER
PUBLISHING COACHING

Patrick Snow has been successfully coaching entrepreneurs on how to get published since 2002. His unique publishing coaching, book promotion coaching, and speaker coaching road map simplifies the process of creating a book and taking it to market. Patrick's system has taken more than 12 years to develop and he currently publishes books for about 50 clients each year. This system includes one-on-one coaching, weekly conference calls, and personal mentoring directly from Patrick Snow. He offers his Best-Seller Publishing Institute at different tropical locales several times a year. See www.BestSellerPublishingCoaching.com for dates and registration information.

Book Publishing:	Patrick's unique road map will take your vision and turn it into a published book within 6 to 18 months. Your book will then serve as a lead-generating tool for your platform that will help grow your speaking, coaching, and consulting practice.
Book Promotion:	Patrick's book marketing program will assist you in creating a best seller. His system will get you into major newspapers, TV, and radio. He will help you find foreign publishers that will help translate your book into numerous languages.
Speaker Coaching:	Patrick's experience as an international keynote professional speaker gives him the knowledge to help you double or even triple your speaker fees. He will share with you his speaking formula that will keep your speaking calendar full.

For a 30-minute, complimentary publishing consultation, contact:

www.BestSellerPublishingCoaching.com

BOOK PATRICK SNOW
TO SPEAK AT
YOUR NEXT EVENT

When it comes to choosing a professional speaker for your next event, you'll find no one more respected or successful—no one who will leave your audience or colleagues with such a renewed passion for life—than Patrick Snow, one of the most gifted speakers of our generation. Since 1986, Patrick has delivered more than 1,500 inspirational presentations worldwide.

Whether your audience is 10 or 10,000, in North America or abroad, Patrick Snow can deliver a customized message of inspiration for your meeting or conference. Patrick understands your audience does not want to be "taught" anything, but rather is interested in hearing stories of inspiration, achievement, and real-life people stepping into their destinies.

As a result, Patrick Snow's speaking philosophy is to humor, entertain, and inspire your audience with passion and stories proven to help them achieve extraordinary results. If you are looking for a memorable speaker who will leave your audience wanting more, book Patrick Snow today.

To see a highlight video of Patrick Snow and find out whether he is available for your next meeting, visit his site below. Then contact him to schedule a complimentary pre-speech interview by phone:

www.PatrickSnow.com
www.CreateYourOwnDestiny.com
Patrick@CreateYourOwnDestiny.com
(800) 951-7721 or (206) 780-1787

INDEX